PLANTS FOR PERFORMANCE

PLANTS
FOR
PERFORMANCE

John Street

with
line illustrations by
Denys Baker

DAVID & CHARLES

NEWTON ABBOT LONDON
NORTH POMFRET (VT) VANCOUVER

ISBN 0 7153 6257 7

Library of Congress Catalog Card Number 74-83320

Set in 11 on 13 pt Bembo and printed in
Great Britain by Ebenezer Baylis & Son Limited
The Trinity Press, Worcester, and London
for David & Charles (Holdings) Limited
South Devon House Newton Abbot Devon

Published in the United States of America
by David & Charles Inc North Pomfret
Vermont 05053 USA

Published in Canada
by Douglas David & Charles Limited
3645 McKechnie Drive West Vancouver BC

CONTENTS

LIST OF ILLUSTRATIONS

INTRODUCTION

What do we want when we start to garden?

We want results—plenty of flowers and good growth. We do not want to waste time and effort learning how to grow something that will be very beautiful—when we find out, by trial and error, just how it should be treated.

This may seem absurdly simple and that a book like this must have been written before. But—not so. The reason is that most gardeners despise the easy plants, largely for that very reason, because they are easy. No skill is required to grow them, they offer no challenge to their knowledge and ability. Furthermore, many knowledgeable horticulturists, and even trained gardeners, would be ashamed to write a book of this kind, because they would be afraid that expert friends might mock its simplicity.

The Nasturtium is the best example of what I mean. It is the first flower that children grow—along with mustard and cress, and radishes. All you have to do is push a seed into the soil—the poorer the better— and up it comes to give a brilliant display of bright orange flowers all through the summer, right on into the autumn, until it is destroyed by frost—and you can even use the leaves for salads.

You cannot fail to grow a Nasturtium—and a Nasturtium never fails to give a show equal to that of many more difficult plants, far better than most. But it is too easy, so it is ignored by the experts.

All the plants in this book are like the Nasturtium—they must grow. They are almost indestructible, and they will be perfectly happy in any good garden soil—acid or lime—with only a minimum of care and attention. There are no 'ifs' or 'buts' about them, and many thrive on neglect.

They are all colourful, gay and exciting, and grow well with little or no maintenance.

9

This is the book for the beginner, because he must succeed with these plants. It is also the book for the lazy gardener who wants a good show of flowers for minimum work. It is also my book—because I like colour and display—and the time to enjoy both, without spending all my spare time in the service of plants which demand constant attention before they bestow their fickle favours.

J.S.

THE PLAN FOR PERFORMANCE

The plants are arranged alphabetically, but there are cross references to particular uses—to flowering periods, colour schemes, height and so on.

For instance, if you find you have a gap in your border in July, you will find a number of shrubs, herbaceous plants and annuals listed under that month. If you want a specimen plant to stand out on its own, all you have to do is look up 'specimen' and make your selection from the plants described—and the same goes for hedging, ground cover, screening and other special positions in the garden.

The common names and the Latin names are included—and cross references are given to these. This has been done because the common names are so much more attractive than the Latin names, although these make the plants easier to find in a nursery catalogue or in a garden centre.

Very simple instructions are included for growing each plant, even though some need the same treatment. This is to save the trouble of having to look them up under another heading. But the next pages give descriptions of what is meant by the various types—annuals, perennials etc—and general tips about sowing and planting.

There are five main types of plant which are our immediate concern —annuals, biennials, herbaceous perennials, shrubs, trees.

Annuals are either hardy or half-hardy. Hardy annuals are the best value of all ornamental plants—six packets of inexpensive seed will fill your garden with colour for three months (the nasturtium is a hardy annual). They are sown directly into the soil, in the places where they are to grow and flower. But they only last for one season. When they are over, the ground must be cleared—ready to be prepared for sowing again next year.

Half-hardy annuals need to be raised in heat under glass. This is a lot of trouble, but many of them give a fine show for a long time. It is simpler and cheaper for the beginner and the lazy gardener to buy plants and set them out after the risk of frost has passed, rather than to go to all the trouble of raising the seedlings, pricking them out and hardening them off.

Biennials flower in the second year of their growth. These may be grown by sowing one year to flower the next—but this involves sowing, thinning, transplanting—exactly the same as with the half-hardy annuals, except that the seeds can be sown outside. It is better for the beginner—and for the man who wants to enjoy his garden without being a slave to it—to buy young plants of biennials which are not expensive.

Perennials, on the other hand, last for ever—in theory. They come up, flower, and die down each year. All those mentioned in this book will do this but, for the sake of good-sized flowers and plenty of them, it pays to lift the clumps every five years, throw away the hard central core, and replant the young vigorous shoots that grow on the outside.

Trees and shrubs are for ever—to all intents and purposes—but you may feel in need of a change after ten years. A tree is very much the same as a shrub or bush—and often the two are available in either form, a tree being called a 'standard'—grown on a single stem with a branching head at the top. A bush throws out branches from the base. Roses are like other trees and shrubs except that they have a shorter life, and are better replaced at least every ten years.

And now—the basic essentials for growing all these.

I would be misleading you if I were to give the impression that they can be sown or planted in virgin soil untouched by human hand. Preparation is essential—and that means digging—turning over the soil with a spade or fork and burying the top weeds.

At the same time, it will help all plants if you mix in something that will put a bit more body into the soil, give them something to feed on—peat, leafmould, spent hops, hop manure, compost or—that commodity that is now becoming rare—farmyard manure. All this should be done as early as possible before planting or sowing, to allow the soil to settle.

Hardy annuals need to have a seed bed made before sowing. This is done by treading down the dug ground and then raking the top to provide what is known as a tilth. This word is almost self-descriptive. It means a layer of well-tilled soil, crumbly and easily worked, with a firm, but not hard, foundation.

Sowing is then simplicity itself. All seeds should go down only as deep as their own size. As the seeds of most of the hardy annuals are very small, it is only necessary to scratch the surface with a pointed stick to make a drill (a shallow furrow) large enough for most annuals. (The nasturtium is the exception here. It has a big seed and you push one in to its own depth, in the place where you want it to grow.) The time for sowing different plants will be given on the packet—but, on the whole, it is better to be a little late than early to make sure the soil is warm.

SOW THINLY—is the advice that is ignored as often as it is given. But remember—thin sowings mean less work in thinning out. This has to be done to remove the excess seedlings, leaving only those at the intervals given on the packets. It is a long and tedious job—so the less there is to do, the better.

Modern methods are beginning to make this job less of a chore. Some small seeds can now be obtained in pelleted form to make it possible to sow them thinly and with precision. The tiny seeds are contained in little balls of clay which you can pick up in your fingers. It is then only necessary to sow twice as many as you need at wide intervals, instead of ten, or twenty or even a hundred more than you can possibly want. For when you do this, you are only making work, not plants. The spares have to be pulled out and thrown away.

Half-hardy annuals (those that are raised under glass and hardened off to a condition that will enable them to live and grow in the open) together with biennials and perennials are all planted where they are to flower, at the times mentioned against the different plants in the alphabetical list. The method is to pull out a small hole in the dug ground, with a spade or trowel, put in the plant, replace the soil—and tread firmly.

The only complication here is with the half-hardy annuals, which are slightly tender and subject to frost damage, and so you must not plant them too early. My advice to anyone who wants to garden for the pleasure of the garden, as opposed to the work it involves, is that it is better to buy these plants than grow them.

The trouble is that many of the shopkeepers and others who sell half-hardy annuals for what is known as 'bedding out' (planting out temporarily for a big show in the summer) are either unscrupulous or ignorant. They try to make you buy them too soon—with the result that the small plants will be killed by a late frost, and you will only have to buy more.

The dates for planting vary from plant to plant and from one part of the country to another. Fortunately, this is now governed by a British Standard Specification—No. 3936: Part 7: 1968, to be exact, and the details are given at the end of this section. There is nothing to be gained by trying to jump the gun on any of the plants mentioned, so do not be tempted, either by a spell of mild weather or a persuasive salesman, to set out your half-hardy annuals too early.

Trees and shrubs—including roses—with bare roots, should first have any damaged roots cut away cleanly with a knife or with secateurs. They should then be planted by taking out a hole deep enough to allow them to be set at the same depth as they were before (with the one exception of roses. These need to go down so that the union of the stock and the bud, which can quite easily be seen, is one inch below the surface of the soil). But only plant in open weather, when there is no frost, and avoid planting in very muddy conditions—better to cover the roots with soil, in a trench, and wait for drier weather.

Do not plant too deeply. More trees and shrubs fail to grow well (they do not actually die) for this reason than any other. When the plant is in the hole, and settled at the right depth, replace the soil, bit by bit, and tread up firmly as you go. When standard trees need a stake, to prevent them being blown out by the wind, put this in the hole before the plant, otherwise the tree may hold up the stake, rather than the other way round.

Do not attempt to spread out the roots of the trees and shrubs which have a tight ball of fibre—like conifers, for instance. They are best left alone, with as little disturbance as possible. The same goes for container grown plants bought from garden centres. Tin or plastic containers should be removed, carefully, when the plant is in the hole, and the roots should only be teased out a little where they may appear to be restricted.

There are a few containers which can be left on the plants—but not many, and it is as well to check with the salesman whether the container may be left as it is, even if it does appear to be perishable.

Now for one or two brief words of wisdom:

Prepare your seed beds and sow the seed when the ground is dry and—believe it or not—during the first phase of a new moon. Do not plant anything in frosty weather or if the ground is very wet—and please remember to prepare the soil well first.

Now—go to it. Follow these simple instructions. Choose any of the plants in the lists, for they are selected for their all-round performance. They will not only enable you to enjoy a beautiful garden in next to no time at all, but they will give you little work or trouble in the future.

	Hardy: Class O	Class A	Class B	Class C
London area	early autumn or March	early April	early May	late May
Manchester	early autumn or March	mid-April	mid-May	early June
Newcastle	early autumn or March	late April	mid-May	late May/ early June
Plymouth	early autumn or March	late March	late April	mid-May
Aberdeen	early autumn or April	late April	late May	early June
Birmingham	early autumn or March	mid-April	mid-May	late May/ early June
Glasgow	early autumn or March	late April	early May	late May/ early June

Note: It cannot be too strongly emphasised that there is no advantage in attempting to beat these dates. Plants set out too early will eventually be outdistanced both in growth and in show of flower by those planted later at the proper time. City areas, coastal belts, and high ground, if not too exposed, can safely be planted a few days before the valleys and inland plains.

Class O hardy	Class A early date	Class B middle date	Class C late date
Aubrieta	Antirrhinum	Alyssum	Ageratum
Alyssum	Calendula	Arctotis	Balsam
saxatile	Carnation	Aster	Begonia
Arabis	Cineraria	Chrysanthemum	semperflorens
Bellis	maritima	(annual)	Calceolaria
Matricaria	Cornflower	Lobelia	Coleus
Myosotis	Larkspur	Mesembryanthemum	Cosmea
Pansy	Pentstemon	Mimulus	Dahlia
Polyanthus	Scabious (annual)	Nemesia	Dimorphotheca
Primrose	Stock (ten week	Nicotiana	Gazania
Silene	bedding)	Petunia	Helichrysum
Stock		Phlox drummondii	Heliotrope
(Brompton)		Sweet William	Impatiens
Sweet William		(annual)	Kochia
('Indian			Marigold
Carpet')			Portulaca
Viola			Salpiglossis
			Salvia
			Tagetes
			Verbena
			Zinnia

Note: All recommendations are made on the assumption that plants have been well hardened-off.

Author's note: I have included all the plants mentioned in the British Standards Specification, although they are not all in this book. The reason for this is that you may feel like trying something else, after you have made a start with the plants that always give a good performance.

THE PLANTS FOR PERFORMANCE

ACHILLEA *filipendula*—Fern-leaf Yarrow
Saucers of yellow flowers from July to August, which may be dried for use in the house in winter. To do this, cut them when they are fully open and hang them up in bunches—upside down—somewhere that is light and airy. The garage is a good place—although some people put them in the bedroom. There are many different varieties, and two of the best are 'Coronation Gold' which grows to 3ft and 'Moonshine', slightly shorter, but with more silvery foliage. Perennial. Buy plants from a nursery or garden centre and set them in the spring.

ACHILLEA *ptarmica*—Sneezewort
This plant sounds as if it received its common name from the spluttering sound of *Ptarmica*, but it comes from the fact that the dry leaves, when crushed, cause you to sneeze—the powder was once used as a substitute for snuff in Scotland. The variety to grow is 'The Pearl'. It carries bobbles of double-white flowers which open in July, and it grows like a weed—in some gardens it can be so vigorous that it has to be kept in check. Incidentally, do not despise white flowers—they show up the other colours, and are cool and refreshing, especially on a hot summer's evening. 2ft. Perennial—buy plants from a nursery or garden centre and set them in the spring.

ACTINIDIA *chinensis*—Chinese Gooseberry
This climbing plant is very late to form its leaves—consequently, it is almost of more use when it is allowed to spread over the ground to cover up the mess left by spring bulbs when they die down, as it is in its conventional role as a climbing plant. The most attractive stage is when the young leaves are expanding as bright red bristly tendrils. Later they become bronzy green and heart shaped. Buy plants, which

must be pot or container grown, from a nursery or garden centre and set them at any time in open weather from the end of September to the end of April.

AGROSTEMMA—see Lychnis *coronaria*

AILANTHUS *altissima*—Tree of Heaven
The most convenient of all trees for any one starting a garden. It grows like Jack's beanstalk for about ten years, then slows down. You can buy it young (which means cheap), plant it—and watch it grow. Ideal for a quick shade tree. It will stand any conditions—and it grows in London as easily as the Plane tree. Another idea with the Tree of Heaven is to buy a young plant, keep it cut back, allow only one shoot to grow each year—and this will throw out enormous leaves, up to 4ft in length, to give a sumptuous, tropical effect. It can be bought either as a young plant, or as a mature specimen, from a nursery or garden centre. Plant in autumn for preference—but this may be done until the end of March, or even later with a plant grown in a container.

ALCHEMILLA *mollis*—Lady's Mantle
Light green leaves shaped like a lady's mantle which hold a drop of dew in the centre, even in the hottest days, feathery yellow flowers in June that fade imperceptibly into attractive seed heads, make this a delightful plant for ground cover—and equally useful for floral decoration. It is so strong growing that I have even known it to fight Ground Elder—and win. Perennial. 1ft high. Buy plants from a nursery or garden centre and set them at any time in open weather from October to April.

ALMOND—see Prunus *communis*

ALSTROEMERIA *aurantiaca*—Peruvian Lily
There are few plants so accommodating as this hardy perennial. It forms a mass of white roots which produce a constant succession of orange flowers throughout the late summer—and the plant is almost indestructible. It can be planted in spring or autumn, and may be bought from most nurseries—but if you have a friend who grows it

already, he or she will be only too pleased to give you a forkful. Do not be misled, at the start, into buying modern versions, like the Ligtu hybrids. These are very beautiful but much more difficult. You can graduate to them later. There is only one point to remember about the Peruvian Lily—if you want to pick the flowers for the house, you must pull them out from the roots—don't cut them. 3–4ft. Perennial. Beg or buy plants and set them in the early spring.

ALYSSUM—the white bedding plant—see Lobularia

ALYSSUM *saxatile*—Mad Wort
The yellow plant which is seen all over the country in the early spring, flowering at the end of April and on through May. It carries a froth

Alchemilla mollis

of yellow blossoms which look particularly well with the mauve of Aubrieta. Alyssum prefers a hot dry spot—and cutting off the flowers as soon as they are finished will help keep it bushy and compact. Do not be tempted into buying the double form because you may think it will give twice as many flowers—it doesn't. 1ft. Dwarf perennial. Buy plants and set them in the spring. (The white annual called Alyssum is correctly named Lobularia—please see.)

AMELANCHIER *canadensis*—Snowy Mespilus
A large shrub or small tree, reaching 10–12ft, which covers itself in white flowers at the end of April. But this is not all—the leaves turn bright orange in the autumn, when it also carries a crop of black berries. It needs a fair amount of room—ultimately a circle of 4 to 6ft in diameter but because of its two displays, in spring and autumn it is worth the extra space. Buy from a nursery or from a garden centre and plant in autumn, if possible, or up to the end of March, if not—but only in open weather. Container grown plants may be planted even later.

AMERICAN CURRANT—see Ribes

ANCHUSA *azurea*—Italian Bugloss
A good blue name for a beautiful blue flower. For many years it was called Anchusa *italica*, and may still be found under that name—which gives the blue a touch of Mediterranean magic. This is a hardy perennial—although there might come a time when you may doubt this to be true. In a very severe winter it may be killed, even into the top root. Do not despair. Mark the spot with a cane, and the long fleshy roots that go down deep will sprout again. There are many varieties, all growing to about 4ft and producing a mass of blue flowers from June right through to August. Two of the best are 'Dropmore' and 'Loddon Royalist'. It is a heavy plant and needs a stake—but it's well worth it. Buy from a garden centre or nursery and set in spring or autumn.

ANEMONE *hupehensis*—Japanese Windflower
This is one of the most delightful plants for the herbaceous border or mixed border in the late summer or early autumn. It has a romantic

origin—for many years the only known sources of this flower were the graves of Chinese Mandarins around Canton, where it was first discovered by Robert Fortune in 1844. Later it was found wild in a remote part of the province of Hupeh—hence the new name. Its chief advantage is that the delicately formed cups make a welcome change from the almost universal daisy pattern of the flowers of late summer and autumn. There are many varieties, ranging from white ('Honorine Jobert') through a semi-double pink ('Max Vogel') to a small flowered red ('Herzblut'). 3 to 4ft. Perennial. Buy plants and set them in the spring.

ANGELICA *archangelica*—Angelica
Strictly speaking this is a herb—it is the plant that provides those green candied stems with a rather intriguing flavour which are used for decorating birthday cakes and the like. But it is a most impressive plant in the garden, something to surprise and startle, both by its flowers and foliage. It has big circles of white flowers above a mass of lush, deep-green leaves, growing to about 4ft. It is fascinating to watch those leaves unfold, slowly expanding and maturing to a majestic beauty. But always cut off the flowers the minute they are over. Never let it set seed. If it does it will die. 4ft. Buy plants—usually to be found in the herb section of a garden centre—and set them in the spring.

APRIL
Alyssum, Amelanchier, Aubrieta, Berberis, Bergenia, Camellia, Chaenomeles, Crocus, Doronicum, Erica, Euphorbia, Forsythia, Kerria *japonica* fl. pl., Lamium, Lunaria, Magnolia, Malus, Muscari, Myosotis, Narcissus, Primula, Prunus, Ribes, Scilla, Tulipa, Vinca.

ASTER—is the Latin name of the Michaelmas Daisy (The half-hardy annual known as the Chinese Aster is another plant—Callistephus *chinensis*.)
Michaelmas Daisies are among the easiest of all plants to grow. The choice ranges from dwarf plants, no taller than 1ft, to giants that grow to 7ft—all flowering in September. Different varieties come in all colours of the rainbow—except yellow. But this can be provided by the later varieties of Golden Rod (Solidago) and the Heleniums. There

are so many Michaelmas Daisies that you could almost take any catalogue and pick them out with a pin. One you should not miss, though, is a very old sort called 'Climax'—a soft mauve flower on dark green foliage. It is so strong that it will survive years of neglect and therefore is the first choice as a performance plant. Another out-of-the-way variety is 'Ericoides' because it has a mass of small off-white flowers, rather like those of a heather. Apart from these, you are safe to take your pick from the trays in a garden centre, or from a nursery catalogue, choosing according to the height and colour. Perennial. Buy plants and set them at any time in open weather from October to April.

AUBRIETA

A trick spelling for a well-known flower—it is usually given an extra 'i' before the final 'a'—'Aubrietia'. This is the dwarf rock plant that flowers so freely in shades of mauve, purple, rosy pink and red at the end of April and in early May. Planted with the yellow Alyssum *saxatile*, it creates one of the many beautiful seasonal variations of that delightful colour scheme—mauve and yellow. As with the Michael-mas Daisies, there are many variations—'Dr Mules', a deep purple, is one of the best known; 'Mrs Rodewald' is red; 'J. S. Baker', a violet mauve with a white eye; and 'Magician' a bright purple. These are all single flowers. There are a few doubles which are better, unlike those of Alyssum, because they last longer: 'Mars' is a double red; 'Mary Poppins', double pink; and 'Greencourt Purple' is a new variety with full double flowers in purple. 1ft at the most. Buy plants and set them in the spring.

AUCUBA—Variegated Laurel

A big-leaved evergreen shrub with foliage splashed with yellow, in different patterns in different forms. This is a shrub that has been in and out of fashion over the years. It was very popular in the days of Queen Victoria, but later it was condemned as being vulgar and garish. Its bright leaves are now much more appreciated because of their use in floral arrangement. The shrub has one great advantage—not only will it grow well in any garden soil, but it will be equally happy in the smoke and grime of industrial areas, because the shiny leaves are soon washed free of soot and grime. 4–6ft. Buy plants from a nursery or garden centre and set them in the early autumn or late spring.

AUGUST

Achillea, Alstroemeria, Anchusa, Anemone, Angelica, Begonia, Buddleia, Calendula, Campanula, Caryopteris, Catananche, Ceanothus, Centaurea, Ceratostigma, Cistus, Clarkia, Colchicum, Coreopsis, Cortaderia, Crocosmia, Delphinium (2nd flowering), Dianthus, Echinops, Echium, Epilobium, Escallonia, Filipendula, Fuchsia, Gaillardia, Galega, Geranium, Geum, Gladiolus, Godetia, Gypsophila, Hebe, Helianthemum, Helianthus, Hemerocallis, Hibiscus, Hydrangea, Hypericum, Inula, Jasmine, Kerria (spasmodic crops), Lathyrus, Lavatera, Lavendula, Leycesteria, Ligularia, Lobularia, Lonicera, Lychnis, Macleaya, Melissa, Nepeta, Olearia, Papaver, Perowskia, Petunia, Phlox, Phygelius, Physalis, Physostegia, Polygonum, Potentilla, Rose, Rudbeckia, Sedum, Senecio, Solidago, Spartium, Tamarix, Tropaeolum, Verbascum, Vinca, Yucca.

AUTUMN CROCUS—see Colchicum

BEGONIAS

As Begonias are considered to be the most difficult of all flowers to grow for exhibition, it may seem surprising that they should be included in this book. But there are Begonias and Begonias. The Belgians, who grow most of the tubers sold in this country, have the easy answer to their cultivation—grow them exactly as you would grow potatoes. Buy the tubers in the spring and set them out in shallow boxes to 'chit'—that is to say, to start into growth. Then plant them in the garden at a suitable time, in most parts towards the end of May, to avoid the risk of frost when the first shoots appear. You can do it earlier, as with new potatoes, if you are prepared to protect the young shoots from late frost. After that, there is nothing to do but enjoy the enormous flowers that they produce in pink, white, yellow, red and orange on plants that grow to about 12–15in in height. If it is possible, they prefer a fairly moist position and somewhere shaded during the hottest part of the day in order that the flowers should last longer. These are known as the 'Tuberous Rooted' Begonias but there are also the varieties and forms of Begonia *semperflorens*, which are sold for bedding out. These are usually bought as plants to be put out in the open garden after risk of frost is past. The table at the beginning of this book shows the different times for the different parts of the country. These make compact little bushes with masses of small pinkish flowers which go on all through the summer. They grow to a height of about 9in. They cannot be kept from year to year, but— just like the potato—the tuberous rooted Begonias can be stored in clamps or anywhere that is frost free, for another show, if they are lifted and cleaned up in the autumn. The flowering period of both is all through the summer. Buy corms or plants and set them as described above.

BERBERIS

There are some people who say they would never have a berberis in the garden on any account—because of their thorns. Yet this would deny some of the most decorative flowering shrubs that can be grown. Berberis *darwinii* is a delightful evergreen growing to about 6 or 8ft and 4 or 5ft wide. It produces orange/yellow flowers towards the end of April and in May. Berberis 'Stenophylla' grows to about the same height and has orange coloured flowers carried on long arching sprays of small dark-green leaves, growing to about the same height. There are many deciduous varieties which are also attractive and the best for autumn colour is Berberis *thunbergii*, green during the summer and bright orange in the autumn. (4–5ft × 4ft.) It has produced a narrow growing form called Berberis *thunbergii* 'Erecta' which will reach about the same height but only 18in through—with the same sort of habit as a Lombardy Poplar. Berberis *thunbergii* 'Atropurpurea' is like the original, but with dark purple foliage—a joy to the flower arrangers—as is the new variety, Berberis *thunbergii* 'Aurea', a beautiful golden form which keeps its colour well.

If you want coral-coloured berries in plenty—then plant Berberis *wilsonae*, which only grows to about 1ft in height and spreads over a wide area—ideal for hanging over a low wall or a position on the rockery. Buy plants from a nursery or garden centre. Set the evergreen varieties in the early autumn or in the spring—the deciduous sorts may be planted at any time in open weather from October to March.

BERGENIA—Pig Squeak or Elephant's Ears

This plant is called by the common name of Pig Squeak because of the noise the leaves make when they are rubbed through the fingers. It is another plant which came into its own through the interest in floral arrangement and it provides large heart-shaped leaves which can form the base for any arrangement. Not only that, but it is an excellent plant for ground cover. Its fleshy evergreen leaves keep down the weeds better than any chemical weedkiller. The flowers appear early in the year, often in March, certainly in April, and they are spikes of pink rather like a giant saxifrage—which, incidentally, it was once called. There are a number of varieties but two of the easiest are Bergenia *cordifolia*, which has green leaves, and its variety 'Purpurea', with leaves that go purple in the winter. It grows to a height of about 1ft and is extremely hardy—which is only natural seeing that it comes from Siberia. Buy plants and set them in the autumn.

BETULA *verrucosa*—Silver Birch

This tree has been rightly called the 'Lady of the Woods'. The Silver Birch is one of our most elegant native trees. In ideal conditions it will grow to a height of 20 or 30ft; it is not long lived, but when young is particularly beautiful and graceful. In a small garden, it would pay to plant a Silver Birch and then, just as it is growing beyond its best, cut it down, use the trunk for firewood and plant another. However, there is a warning about this beauty, if you plant it on the lawn, the grass underneath will suffer. So if you are fussy about your turf, then keep it in a border where it will do no harm. Buy a plant from a nursery in the autumn, or one in a container at any time, and set it in the garden or, hush—you may even lift a seedling from a wild moorland, it would not be missed.

BLUE—Plants, trees, shrubs, with blue flowers

Campanula, Caryopteris, Catananche, Ceanothus, Centaurea, Ceratostigma, Delphinium, Echinops, Echium, Geranium, Hibiscus, Iris, Lavender, Myosotis, Perowskia, Petunia, Phlox, Rosemary, Scilla, Vinca.

BUDDLEIA—Butterfly Bush

Buddleia goes by the delightful common name of the Butterfly Bush for the logical reason that the flowers attract butterflies. There are many different varieties from which to make a choice but there is little need to go into too much detail. Buddleia 'Royal Red' is a dark purple which may not be red but is still a lovely colour—it does, in fact, look red when it is cut and seen under electric light. The whites too are beautiful and the best is 'White Profusion'. There is a variegated form called 'Harlequin' with leaves splashed with cream, and flowers that are reddish-purple, like 'Royal Red'. It is not so strong growing as the others and, perhaps, more suitable for small gardens. Buddleias must be cut down every year in the spring. Treat them almost like perennial plants and chop them hard back to the old wood in March. Then they give beautiful flowers in July and August. There is one other kind that is different from these and it is called Buddleia *globosa*. It forms a big bush, or small tree, about 8 or 10ft high and carries orange/yellow balls in the summer. This will make an unusual specimen, something a little out of the ordinary and it should not be pruned at all. Buddleias are shrubs and should be planted in the autumn, but if they are grown in containers they may be set at almost any time of the year in open weather but—for the best results—not later than the end of May.

CALENDULA—Pot Marigold

Another perfect performance plant. This very easy hardy annual will go on growing, seeding itself every year, always making a contribution from its big orange-yellow flowers. Nowadays there are many sophisticated varieties which begin to look like Chrysanthemums but, as they become naturalised, they revert to the old original type which to my mind is one of the brightest of all our summer flowers. Buy a packet of seed and sow according to the instructions, then weed carefully to save the many seedlings that will come up every year.

CAMELLIA

It might seem a little odd that the Camellia should be included in a list of plants that are very easy to grow—but this is a fact. When camellias first came here they were grown in greenhouses and were

Calendula

considered to be tender plants—but as the greenhouses fell down, because there was not enough money to keep them up, it was discovered that camellias were perfectly hardy, and they are now among the best of our evergreen flowering shrubs. All you need to do for success is to give them a good dose of peat or leafmould when planting and water them when dry. There are two camellias which are foolproof. One is Camellia *japonica* 'Gloire de Nantes', with semi-double pink flowers which often appear in February, and laugh at frost and snow; the other is Camellia 'Williamsii' which flowers in April and even if a frost should take one crop of bloom, there are plenty of buds to follow to give a show for as long as six weeks, come wind, come weather. These both grow to about 6 or 8ft and make excellent evergreen plants as specimens in their own right. Buy plants from a nursery or garden centre, which must be pot grown and—surprisingly —set them in early June when all risk of frost is past, and keep them well watered.

CAMPANULA

These are the perennial Campanulas and there are many different sorts. There are also many colours—but blue is best. 'Gloaming' is a pale blue growing to about 4ft with flowers that are cut like elves' caps. Campanula *lactiflora* 'Pritchards Variety' or 'Loddon Anna' are two that grow to 3–4ft, both blue, flowering in June with heads of flowers, rather than being spread out along the stem. Campanula *pyramidalis*, which reaches 4–5ft and flowers from July to September, is another good blue and there is also a white form. These are all perennials. Buy plants and set them in the spring. Campanula *media* is the Latin name for Canterbury Bells. These are the well known biennials with the cup and saucer flowers in blue, mauve, pink and white. The old fashioned varieties grow to 3ft and need a stake to keep them at their best. There is now a new strain called 'Bells of Holland' which only grows to 15in and needs no staking. The only form of cultivation that is needed—as with many other plants—is to pick off the dead flowers as soon as they have faded, then they will go on giving a good show throughout the summer. Buy plants, set them either in the spring or autumn, and they will flower from June to September giving the delightful ambience of the cottage garden.

CARYOPTERIS 'Clandonensis'

There are few shrubs which give so much for so little. Caryopteris 'Clandonensis' was raised by one of the secretaries of the Royal Horticultural Society, the late Mr A. H. Simmonds in his garden at Clandon, in Surrey, which is how the plant received its name. It forms a small shrub about 2ft high and 3ft across, with grey leaves, and it carries a continuous show of blue flowers from the end of June right through to the autumn. It is not a long lived shrub—say, seven or eight years at the most, but it is well worth replanting. It should be cut down hard in the early spring of every year. Buy plants, which must be pot or container grown, from a nursery or garden centre, and set them in the spring.

CATANANCHE *caerulea*—Cupid's Dart

This hardy perennial was thought by the ancients to be an aphrodisiac, which is the reason for its common name. The best description of the flower is that it is rather like a flattened out cornflower with a silvery back. It will go on throwing these almost throughout the summer, especially if the last blooms of the first flush, which occurs in June, are cut off. It reaches a height of about 2ft and the last flowers can be hung up and dried for use in winter decoration. Buy plants and set them in the spring.

CEANOTHUS

There are two kinds of Ceanothus—evergreen and deciduous—and they each need different treatment. The evergreen varieties are usually grown on a wall, preferably south or west, trained against wires or trellis work. They make an elegant green covering throughout the year and in May they become a sheet of bright blue. The two best varieties to choose are Ceanothus 'Dentatus' and Ceanothus 'Veitchianus'. It is true that the evergreen varieties only just creep into this book on the score of hardiness—for they can be cut to the ground in a really hard winter like that of 1947 or 1963. But not to worry—they shoot again, even more strongly, from the base. Left to grow on their own, as bushes, they will reach about 8ft.

The deciduous Ceanothus are grown as bushes in a shrub or mixed border and go on flowering from the end of June right through to the frosts. There is really only one variety to consider and that is called Ceanothus 'Gloire de Versailles'. It carries crop after crop of powder-blue puff balls of flower which look particularly well if planted near to a yellow-flowering shrub—for example, Hypericum 'Hidcote'. There is one small point of cultivation that is important for the deciduous Ceanothus—they should be pruned in the same way as a Hybrid Tea Rose, by cutting back the old wood in the spring to the second or third growth bud—they will then grow to about 4–5ft. Buy plants from a nursery or garden centre. They must be grown in pots or in containers for they will not transplant from open ground. Set the deciduous varieties at any time in open weather from October to April, but the evergreens preferably in the spring.

CENTAUREA

Centaurea *cyanus* is the high-class name for the Cornflower which is very much a performance plant, as good as the Nasturtium, and delightful when planted near it. Nowadays you can have Cornflowers in almost any shape or colour you wish, tall, short, medium—pink, blue, mauve, purple, white. But to my mind the Cornflower is always blue—and blue it should remain. (I am so old fashioned that I happen to know it is the buttonhole to wear if you are driving a horse and trap or a coach and four. Why? I just don't know.) It is an annual plant; buy seeds and sow them according to the instructions in the beginning of this book—and they are now available in pelleted form which saves much time and bother. A spring sowing in March will give flowers in June, a later sowing in May will give flowers in September—you can choose the height from 9–12in up to 2–3ft according to the varieties offered by the seedsmen. Centaurea *dealbata* is the first cousin of the Cornflower but it is perennial. Even so, it gives just as good value, if not better. The plants will go on giving flowers year after year once they have become established. Its foliage is attractive—being grey on top, covered with a fine down, and silver underneath. The flowers are like exaggerated Cornflowers which have something of the character of a thistle. The colour is purple and they are red at the base. The plant grows to a height of about 12–18in. The trick is to have two or three clumps in a group, and cut some down as soon as they start to flower. These will come into bloom when the others finish—giving a succession from early June, or even late May, right on to September. The dark reddish-purple colour of the base is taken up very attractively by Geranium *sanguineum* if it is planted nearby. Perennial. Buy plants from a nursery or garden centre and set them in the spring.

CERATOSTIGMA *willmottianum*

This is technically a shrub although it behaves like a perennial—as it dies back to the base every year, even at the slightest hint of frost. But it comes up again, happily, in the spring, sometimes sprouting from the old growth, depending upon the severity of the winter. Even so, it is better to cut it all away at the end of March and start afresh. It then grows to about 18in or 2ft and gives a mass of blue flowers that really are blue. It can be planted in a border or on the rock garden, and the poorer the soil, the hotter the spot—the better it likes it. Buy plants which should be pot grown, and set them in the spring.

CHAENOMELES—Japanese Quince—Japonica

So many good plants have come to us from Japan, that the one known as the Japonica (meaning the Japanese Plant) should be good—and it is. The Japonica is very much a cottage garden plant and can often be seen flowering to perfection on walls of old houses and, occasionally, from stray seedlings peeping through hedgerows. It is particularly beautiful in the early spring. It will start flowering in March going on through April and May, with spasmodic flowers throughout the summer. Although it is often seen growing on a wall, it can be planted as a shrub, for it is not a natural climber. The best known varieties are those that produce bright orange-scarlet flowers. These are 'Knaphill Scarlet', 'Cardinalis' and 'Rowallane Seedling'. They have strong upright growth which can be trained against a wall, if desired. The oldest of all is one now called Chaenomeles *japonica*, but is still well known as Cydonia *maulei*. This is probably the true Japonica. It is more compact in growth reaching 2–3ft as compared with the others 4–5ft and is better planted on its own to be allowed to spread by suckers. It has one of the brightest orange-red flowers of them all. Chaenomeles 'Moerlesii' is also known by the common name of Apple Blossom, because this is the colour of the flowers—pink and white. Chaenomeles 'Nivalis' is a pure white which can be very attractive against a red wall. All of them are easy, but they benefit from being pruned after they have finished flowering, and then being tipped back at the end of July or early August. This is probably why they look so well on cottage gardens because, more often than not, the shears are run over them at the same time as the hedges are cut. They all produce big, quincelike fruits, which make excellent jelly—said to be like the guava jelly made in the West Indies. Buy pot or container grown plants and set them at any time in open weather from October to April.

CHAMAECYPARIS—False Cypress

The true Cypress, in classical gardening, is the Italian Cypress—the tall, straight tree that framed the views from the Renaissance gardens of Italy. But the 'False Cypress' comes from America, China and Japan. And there is probably no plant which has produced so many different varieties of Cypresses as Chamaecyparis *lawsoniana*, which grows naturally in the States of Oregon and California in western America. The variety which most closely resembles the image of the Italian Cypress is Chamaecyparis *lawsoniana* 'Erecta Viridis', which grows to 20ft in time. The long name indicates an evergreen tree which has the typical 'Candle-Flame' shape associated with the Italian Cypress. It makes an excellent specimen, on its own; while a pair will set off a drive or path very elegantly. A new form, which can be used for a similar purpose, has recently been introduced. It is called Chamaecyparis *lawsoniana* 'Columnaris' and grows straighter, to about the same height, but without the delicately rounded curve of C. *lawsoniana* 'Erecta Viridis'. It is grey-blue instead of green. The choice would depend on the particular situation in the garden where they are to be planted to give that classical air of old-world formality. Chamaecyparis *lawsoniana* 'Fletcherii' is a useful plant because it can easily be adapted to different forms. If a narrow tree is required, the side shoots can be pinched out, with finger and thumb, to keep it growing in a narrow pyramid shape. But if it is allowed to grow naturally, it will develop several leading shoots that will give it a more comfortable, buxom outline. It has finely-cut silver-grey leaves, which make an excellent foil to other plants; and in ten years it will reach 8 or 9ft from a small 18in shrub. Chamaecyparis *lawsoniana* 'Ellwoodii' is

Crocus 'Queen of the Blues'—
One of the great assets of the large flowered crocus is that it can be obtained in yellow, white, purple and blue. All of these colours go well together, so that you cannot go wrong colour-wise with the crocus

Crocus yellow—
A yellow form of the dwarf Crocus chrysanthus. *There are many named varieties which have a charm of their own, rivalling that of their big brothers*

Primrose—
Primroses are now available in many colours. In fact, it is easier to buy pinks, reds and mauves than the true natural yellow

similar in appearance—C. *l.* 'Fletcherii' might be its big brother. The interesting point about C. *l.* 'Ellwoodii' is that you will often find it classified in catalogues as a 'rock garden conifer'. This is only partly true. For the idea of a 'rock garden conifer' is one that remains dwarf and compact, seldom growing more than 4ft. But C. *l.* 'Ellwoodii', if it is planted in good garden soil, with plenty of room for its roots to develop—as opposed to the somewhat constricted space in a rock garden—will grow to a perfect specimen of silver grey, at a height of about 8–10ft, and stay there. This makes it a very useful conifer to provide a focal point of attraction in a small garden. There are many golden forms of the 'False Cypress' and they have a particular value in giving colour to the garden in late autumn and during the winter—they are at their best in November. Chamaecyparis *lawsoniana* 'Lutea' has the brightest golden foliage of all. It will, in time, reach 20 or 30ft—but that will be a very long time. All the while it will provide colour in the winter from its bright yellow leaves, which look as if they are basking in the sunlight even when skies are grey. The best of the really dwarf forms for the rock garden is Chamaecyparis *lawsoniana* 'Minima Glauca'. This grows into a rounded bush with neat whorls of foliage in grey green.

Two or three of these conifers—tall, medium or dwarf—will literally make a garden. They create the vertical framework around which the rest of the design may be planned. Buy plants, either from the open ground or in containers, and set them at any time in open weather from October to March.

CHRYSANTHEMUM

If you have ever been to a Chrysanthemum show and seen those enormous flowers, like shaggy sheep dogs, which are produced by the experts, you might wonder why any of them should be included in this book. But there are Chrysanthemums and Chrysanthemums. Those highly cultivated hothouse beauties are all very well in their place—on the show bench—but when it comes to garden decoration, or flower decoration, the 'Sprays' and the 'Koreans' and the 'Hardy Chrysanthemums' are much more useful.

The 'Korean Chrysanthemums' were first introduced into Britain in the early 1930s by way of America. They are all hardy varieties which grow to a height of 2–4ft, depending on the situation and, for the most part, they are single flowers in good chrysanthemum colours of bronze, near red, pink and yellow. New varieties are raised by the 100 and, if any were listed, the list would be out of date before this book is in print. There are one or two which will live on—like 'Wedding Day', an excellent white, 'Jante Wells', a compact, neat yellow, and 'Rosalie', a very late flowering pink which will withstand up to 7° of frost in December, and 'Lammas Day', a bronze—but it is as well to see what is currently available at a nursery or garden centre, and make your own choice. Then there are the hardy sprays which caused the late Mrs Constance Spry to say that you can do nothing with a big disbudded large flowered chrysanthemum, but everything with a spray. One of the best is a yellow called 'Golden Orfe' and, very like it, but slightly deeper in colour, 'Lilian Hoek'. Both of these can be planted outside to grow with the same lack of attention as a Michaelmas Daisy. The 'Rubellum' Chrysanthemums are the strongest growing of all, and the best is a rich pink called 'Clara Curtis'. It looks particularly well when planted near Aster 'Frikartii', a little known Michaelmas Daisy which is mauve and blue and short growing.

It may not be generally known that one of our own weeds is a chrysanthemum, the 'Ox Eye Daisy'. This can be a useful plant for cutting, but there are many better flowers to be found in a similar plant, Chrysanthemum *maximum*, which is found in the Pyrénées. The best known of all is a variety called 'Esther Read'—it has the distinction of being known by this name in all the flower markets of Britain. It has a full double clear-white flower from June to August and grows to about 1½–2ft. There are many other forms of Chrysanthemum *maximum* worth growing: 'Beauté Nivelloise', is a single with frilly white flowers, cut at the ends of the petals, with a golden centre; 'Wirral Pride' is a pure white with an anemone centre and 'Snow Princess' is a double flowered variety with fringed petals like 'Beauté Nivelloise'. These are all perennials—buy plants and set them in the spring.

CISTUS

There are few summer flowering evergreen shrubs, but the Cistus is one of them. It has another valuable quality—it does not produce its flowers in one glorious burst, but goes on giving them throughout the late summer. Like the Ceanothus, it can be killed to the ground, even killed outright, in a very bad winter—but it is so good, that it is worth the risk. Cistus 'Corbariensis' is the most useful. It forms a small round compact bush about 2ft high and 3ft across with bronzy-green leaves, and it produces white flowers, 1½in wide, which tend towards yellow at the base of the petal. For a tall shrub, up to 8ft, plant Cistus 'Cyprius' or either of its parents—Cistus 'Ladaniferus' or Cistus 'Laurifolius'. The first two have a dark blotch at the base of the petal, which makes them particularly attractive, while Cistus 'Laurifolius' is pure white shading to a creamy-yellow base. Cistus 'Laurifolius', incidentally, is the hardiest of all, while Cistus 'Ladaniferus' is the source of the drug laudanum, which is gathered by whipping the bushes and scraping the gum off the thongs of the whips. There are many pink forms but most of them are tender, miffy and difficult. There is one with grey leaves, called Cistus 'Crispus', which is a reliable hardy plant—at least in my experience. But you pay for the hardiness in the somewhat coarse colour of the flower which, to be honest, is magenta or puce pink. But you cannot have everything. An evergreen shrub that grows to 3ft and flowers in summer is not to be despised. The fact that it grows naturally in Spain, Portugal and the South of France and has been grown here in gardens since 1656, if not earlier, gives some idea of its resilience. Buy plants, which must be pot or container grown, and set them in the spring.

CLARKIA

This is another 'Nasturtium' plant, a hardy annual as foolproof as it is beautiful. You cannot go wrong with Clarkia. It is a hardy annual that is so easy to grow, that a packet of seed will produce enough plants to decorate a whole village. This is the only danger—if ordinary seed is sown it must be thinned out ruthlessly. Fortunately, this very decorative—typical cottage-garden, teacosy plant—can now be bought as pelleted seed, and the extra cost is well worth the saving in time and labour. There is only one point worth remembering about Clarkia, when selecting packets of seed from a stand in a garden shop or garden centre or when ordering them from a seedsman—the mixed collections are not really worth having. They contain so many forms that are

Clarkia

either bluey-pinks or pinky-blues that they can be offensive. It is better, if you can, to choose pure colour strains—like salmon or pink—but you may not be able to have these in pelleted form.

CLEMATIS

Clematis are beautiful climbing plants which are well known—but those great big flowers are too temperamental for this book. They are all liable to die suddenly, for no apparent reason—although that reason may well be Clematis Wilt, an unfortunate disease for which no adequate cure has yet been found. Not only that, they also demand all sorts of other complications—like their roots in the shade and their tops in the sun and intricate systems of pruning for each variety. However, there are some Clematis that do give a good performance, both in flower and behaviour. The most decorative are the forms of Clematis *montana*, a strong growing climber with a mass of white flowers. It will clamber over your garden shed to give a glorious show of flower in May. This has a pink form, called 'Rubra' (which is a slight exaggeration, for 'rubra' means red). And there is now a larger flowered variety which has been named 'Tetra'. All these three can be planted and left to grow without trouble—until they become so robust that they need to be kept in check. Even stronger, is our native Clematis—Traveller's Joy—Clematis *vitalba*. This, perhaps, is more beautiful in the winter, in its fluffy seed heads, than it is in the spring for its small white flowers. It is a curious plant of considerable charm— it grows well on any type of soil yet it has a slightly exotic, junglelike appearance with its long vigorous strands, like some climbing plant dropping down from the luxuriant growth of a tropical forest.

CLIMBING PLANTS

The following list only includes those plants that will climb up a support on their own with a little help. Those that need training and tying to make them into wall plants are listed under that heading: Actinidia, Clematis, Fatshedera, Hedera, Hydrangea, Jasmine, Lathyrus, Lonicera, Polygonum, Rose, Tropaeolum, Vitis.

COLCHICUM—Autumn Crocus

This is not to be confused with the Autumn Flowering Crocus which is a totally different plant. The Autumn Crocus is a plant with considerable power. It is the source of the material called colchicine which has been used as a cure for rheumatism and can even change the genetic structure of plants, in exactly the same way as if they were treated with atomic rays. Even so, the Autumn Crocus is a delightful plant which is not used nearly as much as it should be. The reason for this is that it needs to be ordered and planted much earlier than other bulbs. The latest time at which it should be put into the ground is the end of July. Buy bulbs and plant in the spring or summer.

COREOPSIS *verticillata*

This perennial has two forms of beauty—attractive, finely cut leaves in rich green and successive crops of yellow, daisy-shaped flowers from June to September. It is also compact growing, making about 18in or 2ft, and needs no staking. It should be placed towards the front of the border and it is best to buy plants from a nursery or garden centre and set them in the spring.

CORNUS—Dogwood

There are several different kinds of Dogwood—one of them even grows wild in our own woods and hedgerows—and they vary from big trees to a tiny creeping plant which is one of the most difficult of all to grow.

There are two that measure up to the title of being performance plants. They are both equally attractive and useful in their different ways.

Cornus *alba* 'Elegantissima' has red stems in the winter (those right inside the bush, in the shade, become bright coral pink) and these are covered with brightly variegated leaves—silver and green—in the summer. It is a very striking plant growing to about 5ft and needs placing carefully in a position where it will not be too bright for its surroundings.

Cornus *Mas* is one of our oldest cultivated ornamental plants. It is known as the Cornelian Cherry because it carries small plumlike fruits which resemble Cornelians. Many years ago it was grown in orchards for the sake of these somewhat bitter fruits. But it is now of more interest as an ornamental plant making a large bush or small tree up to 8ft. It will produce a crowd of small starlike yellow flowers very early in the year—often in January—and it is still able to hold its own with the many other winter-flowering shrubs that are now available. Its secondary beauty is in the somewhat angular growth that makes it curiously attractive even when it is without flowers or leaves. Buy young shrubs from a nursery or garden centre and plant at any time in open weather from October to March.

COROKIA

Part of the attraction of the shrub called Corokia *cotoneaster* is similar to that of Cornus *Mas*—black stems that are twisted and wiry. These carry small silver leaves at fairly wide intervals which make an intriguing effect that is faintly reminiscent of a modern painting of a flowering shrub. It is decorative in its form and habit rather more than for the small yellow flowers. These are a little larger in the other species, Cotoneaster *virgata,* but this lacks the interest of the strange habit of Corokia *cotoneaster.* Both grow to about 4ft. Buy plants, which must be pot or container grown, from a nursery or garden centre and set them in the spring.

CORTADERIA—Pampas Grass

The stately blooms of the Pampas Grass, 6 or 8ft tall, were seen almost too often in the gardens of the mid-thirties. It became as much a centre piece of the front lawns of suburban houses as the Monkey Puzzle was in Victorian times. There was then a reaction and the Pampas Grass was left severely alone. But it is undoubtedly a plant which gives a sumptuous effect for a long time for no trouble. The plumes may be dried and used for winter decoration, provided they are thrown out when they become too dusty. Buy plants from a nursery garden and set them in the spring—but only in the spring, and the best variety, if you can obtain it, is 'Sunningdale Silver'.

CORYLUS *maximum* 'Atropurpureum'—Purple Leaved Nut

One of our most beautiful trees is the purple leaved Beech but there are few gardens today which can hope to plant one and see it reach maturity. A very good substitute, on a small scale, is the Purple Leaved Nut. It grows into a rounded shrub, up to about 10ft high by as much through, and its foliage is as good as the Purple Beech, if not a little better. Large heart-shaped leaves are dark purple. Buy plants and set them at anytime in open weather from the end of October to the end of March—they may be from the open ground or in containers.

COTONEASTER

There are two ways of pronouncing this name—you can either call it Cot-tone-é-aster or you can call it Cotton-easter—but the first is generally preferred. Methods of pronunciation are unimportant compared with the enormous variety of plants that are contained in the different species and hybrids of this shrub. They start, very small, with one called Cotoneaster *microphylla* 'Thymifolia'. This is a creeping shrub with leaves described by the name—similar to those of Thyme. Going up, one of the best known is Cotoneaster *horizontalis*, the Herringbone Cotoneaster. This can either be grown as a climbing plant on a wall, as a ground cover plant or at the edge of a bank or on a rockery. It has a spreading habit with a branch formation like the bones of a herring. These are covered with green leaves which turn bright scarlet in the autumn to match the berries which it bears freely. It will not climb right up the walls of the house, but it is ideal for covering up beneath the window in a hot dry position. All that is necessary is to plant it near to the wall and it will turn up against it quite naturally. For an evergreen that bears white flowers and large red berries, there is little to beat Cotoneaster *conspicuus* 'Decorus' a medium sized shrub, growing to about 3ft and then trailing its branches on to the ground. For its form alone and the beauty of its habit it is worth planting. Then there are what are known as the Watererii group. This name comes from the first hybrid which is called Cotoneaster 'John Waterer', a tall growing shrub which can, if wished, be trained as a standard tree. It has evergreen leaves and large red berries—these last right through the winter, even after Christmas, because the birds seem to dislike them. Another, very similar, is Cotoneaster 'Cornubia'—and there is not much to choose between the two. The third, Cotoneaster 'Exburyiensis', is a yellow-berried form with rather more spreading branches. All are attractive and useful for screening an eyesore. Buy plants from a nursery or garden centre, set them at any time in open weather from the end of October to the end of March. The first three must either be pot or container grown. The last three should be container grown or supplied with a root ball of soil and fibre held together for transport by a canvas covering.

CROCOSMIA—Montbretia

If you read a dictionary of gardening, or a gardening book that deals with small bulbs, you may be given the impression that Montbretia is a somewhat difficult plant. It is not. It is one of the easiest of all. It is often seen growing rampantly in London gardens in deep shade and flowering profusely with its orange/red flowers in August. It is useful for the late summer because it gives a different type of flower from the daisies which seem to dominate the garden scene then. It produces a new bulb on top of the old and it is quite safe to leave this to mature, with the old one to die underneath, but it does help to replant every three or four years. There are one or two varieties that are worth noting. The most popular, at the present time, is 'Masonorum', which has bright orange, scented flowers, 'His Majesty', an older variety with a lighter centre, and 'Mrs Heggarty', a pink. Buy bulbs and set them at any time from September to February.

CROCUS

Of all the small bulbs which, it is sad to say, are somewhat neglected, the Crocus—in its different forms—offers the greatest reward for the least labour. With a little care—and it is very little—the big flowered varieties, the best known, will give colour for six weeks or more. The trick is to plant a group at different depths. Some at 2in, some at 4in and some at 6in. This is all against the advice given in the books, but it does change their period of flowering so that in any one group the flowers will come out in succession. The large flowered crocuses can be bought very cheaply in mixed collections but you may have a preponderance of purples and whites and few yellows—or all yellows. This is apt to be boring. Consequently, it does pay to spend a little more and buy individual varieties. 'Purple Beauty' is a deep purple and 'Yellow Giant' is good for that colour. 'Queen of the Blues' (see page 33) is a pale lilac, 'White Lady' is the best white. But there are many more, and the good named varieties are, more or less, as good as one another. But it is worth remembering that with small bulbs, the cheapest are often the best—the reason for this is that they are the varieties that increase more quickly.

There are also the small crocuses, both species and hybrids, which have an even greater charm because of their dwarf habit and the fact that the flowers start as typical chalice-shaped buds and then open to something that looks rather like a miniature water lily. Perhaps the best of these are the different forms and varieties of the species called Crocus *chrysanthus* (see page 34). 'Cream Beauty' is a pale creamy yellow with a bright orange centre. 'E. A. Bowles' is deep yellow with grey markings at the base, 'Marion' is royal purple outside and creamy white at the edge, the inside of the petal is yellow and the centre is orange. 'Snow Bunting' is a white. Or you can buy mixed seedlings which will, in fact, give a wide variety of flowers because they are seedlings—and not just spare bulbs jumbled up together to make a collection, as with the mixed offers of the large flowered varieties.

There is a third range of spring flowering crocus, nearly all of which are worth growing, different species that have not become well known. Crocus *susianus* 'Cloth of Gold' is grey outside and yellow inside when it is in bud—opening to starlike yellow flowers at maturity. But perhaps the best of all of these, so far as this book is concerned, is Crocus *tomasinianus* which is a lilac flowered crocus and almost a weed. It grows anywhere and everywhere and will seed itself to become naturalised in many gardens—particularly those where the owner is careful to leave the seedlings when taking out the weedlings. Buy bulbs and plant in September.

Then there are the autumn flowering species which include Crocus *stylus*, the species that produces saffron, and from which Saffron Walden gets its name. It has purple-pink flowers striped with deeper purple. Saffron is obtained from the stamens in the centre and, I presume, it may be possible to obtain your own stock of this very expensive spice from Crocus *stylus*. Crocus *speciosus* is lavender blue, with yellow anthers and an orange centre. 'Oxonian' is a darker blue. Crocus *nudiflorum* is lilac mauve, comes from the Pyrénées and has become naturalised on the hills around Carlisle. These are just a few examples of the autumn flowering crocuses which must not be confused with the Autumn Crocus (Colchicum). They need to be planted in the spring or early summer—which is why they are often over-looked, even by those who appreciate the beauty and display of small bulbs.

CUPRESSOCYPARIS 'Leylandii'

This tree might well be called the marvel of the age—it is the fastest growing conifer of them all, putting on as much as 4ft a year when it is established. It is the perfect plant for the quick screen, yet it is not greedy and takes little out of the ground. It forms a typical Italian Cypress shape, rather like that of a candle flame—but not quite so classically moulded as that of Chamaecyparis *lawsoniana* 'Erecta Viridis'—and in a dark olive-green colour. There is only one danger with this plant. It will throw a double leader without you noticing it. That is to say, the main trunk will divide but this will not be apparent because the two leading branches will be so close together as to appear to be one. Unfortunately, when these two have grown fairly tall, a strong wind can blow one out, leaving a bare side to the tree. Therefore, the only attention that is necessary to this useful tree—and it is very necessary—is to be certain that it goes up with one solitary leading shoot. Any rival must instantly be removed. Buy plants, which must either be pot or container grown, and set them in the early autumn or in the spring.

CYTISUS—Broom

It is quite remarkable how the Common Broom—officially known as Cytisus *scoparius*—the plant that grows in profusion on our commons and moors, has produced so many beautiful garden plants. They can now be had in almost any colour, even blue, or rather, a mauve that is very close to blue. There is 'Burkwoodii', a red; 'Windlesham Ruby', another; 'Andreanus', yellow and red; 'Criterion', orange and yellow; 'Geoffrey Skipwith', a pink; 'Killiney Salmon'; and the variety that begins to touch the edge of blue—the mauve 'Mrs Norman Henry', and many more. Buy plants from a nursery, they must be in pots, and they must be on their own roots—make sure of this. There is one very important point of cultivation—cut them hard back, to within an inch of the young growth, as soon as they have finished flowering. In this way, the broom becomes a delightful flowering shrub at about 3 or 4ft, giving joy throughout May and into June. But if you leave them they will grow to ungainly monsters of 8ft, all dead wood and blackened stem with a few unseen spasmodic flowers at the tops of their branches.

These are the varieties of the common broom but there are others. There is one, for instance, called Cytisus 'Praecox' which needs no pruning. It forms a beautiful shrub with grey stems that weep down rather in the manner of a miniature Weeping Willow. It has very pale yellow flowers in the early spring—usually at the beginning of May or sometimes earlier, and a delightful peppery scent, similar to that of a Lupin.

The Portugal Broom (Cytisus *albus*) is also useful because it can be planted among other shrubs and perennials and anywhere—for that matter—to give a display of its white flowers in the late spring, high above the other plants, to show them off. The beauty of this plant is that it takes very little out of the soil and does no harm to the plants that surround it. So place it somewhere where it can make a powerful contribution to the general display, more as a crowd player in the scene, than anything else. Like the others, it must be a pot grown shrub because brooms do not move easily from the open ground. They may be planted at almost any time of the year in open weather, but the autumn is to be preferred.

There is one other form of the Cytisus that should be mentioned as being up to the standard required by this book—Cytisus *virgata*. This is a late summer flowering species which grows to about 8 or 10ft. It makes an excellent specimen, and it carries its scented yellow flowers in August. The foliage is slightly touched with silver and even when it is out of flower, it is a very elegant plant. Buy plants from a nursery or garden centre which, I repeat, must be on their own roots, and they must be pot or container grown. Set them at any time from the end of October to the middle of April in open weather.

DAFFODIL—see Narcissus

DAYLILY—see Hemerocallis

DECEMBER

Some species and varieties of the following plants flower in December, or they have attractive bark or berries during that month: Betula, Cornus, Cotoneaster, Hamamelis, Ilex, Jasminum, Leycesteria, Lonicera, Lunaria, Mahonia, Physalis, Prunus, Pyracantha, Viburnum.

DELPHINIUM

This plant, like several more in this book, is almost too well known to need detailed description. It might be thought, by those who have seen the magnificent displays of enormous spikes at the Chelsea Flower Show, that it did not qualify to be included, because of the apparent difficulty of growing and the need for constant staking and attention. But this would be a mistake. The best way of finding the Delphiniums suitable for your own garden is to buy—or grow— some mixed seedlings. It will then be found that some of these will be much more suitable than others—both as to size of spike, colour of flower and, perhaps even more important, in their performance in the soil and climate of a particular garden. Having found these, and selected the best—both for colour and constitution, keep them, and care for them. They can then be divided in the spring, a simple opera- tion of splitting up the roots to take growing shoots with some root attached—in order to increase the stock of those that are preferred, and which also prefer the conditions you have to offer.

But the Delphinium has been cut down to size in recent years. The 'Belladonnas' only grow to about 3 or 4ft, and they do not require staking or, at least, only the minimum support of a few peasticks. And there are many excellent varieties in this particular strain. 'Capri' is sky blue at between 3 and 4ft, 'Lamartine' is violet blue at 4ft, 'Moer- heimii' is a pure white rising to between 3 or 4ft, 'Pink Sensation' is a light rose pink at about the same height—but, probably the best of all, is 'Wendy', a deep blue with a white eye at 3½ft.

If you do want height, and are prepared to give your Delphiniums the benefit of a stake, then 'Charles F. Langdon', a medium blue with a black eye, 'Fred Yule', purple and blue with a black eye, and 'Swan Lake', white with a black eye, grow up to 6ft in good conditions.

Technically, the Larkspur is a Delphinium—the hardy annual form of that plant. But, of course, to many people it will still be better known as the Larkspur. Yet—more than that—Larkspur means blue, and you would be surprised how difficult it is to buy a packet of seeds of a true blue Larkspur! You can obtain all sorts of colours from pink, almost red, to white but plain blue Larkspur just doesn't seem to be fashionable any more. It may be prejudice on my part, but I feel that Larkspur should be blue—like the Cornflower. Even so, it does not matter all that much about the colour—because it is a very decorative flower. It has a considerable value, so far as this book is concerned, because Larkspur is one of the few plants—one might almost say the only plant—that will grow happily in the roots of a privet hedge. Normally, a privet hedge is greedy. It takes so much out of the soil that it is almost impossible to grow anything within 4ft of it—not the Larkspur.

DEUTZIA

The Deutzias are shrubs which may be big and coarse—even ugly— but there are three which are particularly choice and graceful. Deutzia 'Gracilis' is a small growing plant which will produce a display of white flowers, in singularly dainty form, at the end of May or the beginning of June. There is a variety called 'Hillierii' which has pink flowers and is similar in appearance, and another called 'Kalmiaflora', with those beautifully formed blossoms, like the Kalmia, which look like miniature umbrellas or parachutes, or the flowers that are used to decorate iced cakes. This last variety has a great advantage over the true Kalmia—it can be grown on any soil, acid or lime, poor or rich. All of these three reach about $3\frac{1}{2}$–4ft and should be pruned immediately after they have flowered. Buy plants from a nursery or garden centre and set them at any time in open weather from the end of October to the end of March.

DIANTHUS

This is the Latin name of the Carnation, the Pink and the Sweet William. First of all—the Carnation. There was a time, some years ago, when there were hardy Carnations which would grow and flower as easily as Michaelmas Daisies—and keep on flowering. But these seem to have dropped out of cultivation and it is almost impossible to buy the plants so, unfortunately, I cannot recommend them. The only possibility is to grow the easy seedling forms like 'Enfant de Nice', from which it is just possible to select some which may prove to be

48

Dianthus 'Doris'

perennial in your own garden. Do not have any truck with the so-called Border Carnations. These only give their flowers for a very short period and, if they are to be at their best, need careful treatment.

The Pinks are a different matter and come well into the scope of this book. Probably the best known of them all is the old double-flowered white variety with the fabulous scent, called 'Mrs Simkins'—raised by the wife of the workhouse keeper in Slough, late in the nineteenth century, and it now forms part of the arms of that borough. There are others, nowadays, which are much better because they give a long period of flower, instead of just one great glorious show. The best of all is a Pink called 'Doris'—a deep salmon with a faintly darker rim in the centre of the petal. Then there are the London Pinks, which are deeply marked with dark stripes round the edges of the flowers together with a blotch in the centre, and the 'Allwoodiis' and the 'Highland' Pinks. Many varieties, particularly the Allwoodiis, will go on flowering into the late autumn. It is just possible that these might be obtainable from garden centres, as grown plants, otherwise, it is necessary to buy seed, grow your own, and select those which suit you and your garden best—rather like the Delphiniums. But there is one point that is well worth remembering here—I have had a plant of one of the old Highland Pinks growing in the middle of a hardy geranium—and the two seem to enjoy each other's company so much that they grow better than if they were living in splendid isolation.

The Sweet Williams are biennials—and well known. They need the normal, biennial treatment which, to my mind, is more simply applied by buying the plants and setting them rather than by growing your own. They will give flower over a long period, some are scented —but nothing to be compared with the Pink or the Carnation—yet, quite apart from that, they give very good garden value, particularly if they are 'dead-headed', which means the removal of the flowers that have faded.

DIGITALIS—Foxglove

A wild, native plant which has been improved out of all recognition— larger flowers, better presentation, taller spikes, more varied colour (see page 51). It is best treated as a biennial but it is possible for some plants to develop a tough constitution which will enable them to carry

Foxglove—
The Foxglove is a wild native plant which has been groomed for stardom. The best of the modern varieties rival many exotic plants in their beauty

Gaillardia—
The Gaillardia is known as the Blanket Flower, probably because its sharp contrast of dark red and yellow is similar to the colour of the blankets of the Navajo Indians, in whose country it grows wild

Hemerocallis—
The Daylily (Hemerocallis) has been transformed in the last twenty years. Plant breeders in America and in this country have raised so many new hybrids from the original yellow form that it is now possible to have any colours from mahogany red to mauve

Kerria *japonica* fl. pl.—
The Jews Mallow (Kerria japonica fl. pl.*) is a success story among flowering shrubs. Within thirty-five years of its introduction it was being grown everywhere, even in the smallest cottage gardens. Called Jews Mallow because it resembles a Corcorus which Jews once ate as a vegetable*

on flowering for two or three years. Even the wild plant is not to be despised. The spike and the flower are smaller than in the cultivated varieties, but it can often have an intense colour of rich purple red which is lacking in the more sophisticated forms. The most impressive are the 'Excelsior' hybrids. They have spikes up to 6 or 7ft, and these are so strong that they will stand on their own without staking. The flowers are in attractive pastel colours—soft mauves, lilacs, creams— and so on. But the considerable advantage they have over the common variety is that they are spaced all round the stem, not on one side. These hybrids, if treated kindly, will become naturalised in the garden, and so save the work of sowing and replanting. The only attention they need is that they should not be plucked out and thrown away with the weeds. Fortunately, the leaves—which are thick and fleshy, grey-green colour, forming a small rosette, are easy to recognise. But it has to be admitted that, after about five years, these self-sown seedlings deteriorate a little from the original beauties. Consequently, it is advisable, at this stage, to grub them all out—and start again with a fresh set. A new form has recently been introduced from America called 'Foxy'—again in mixed pastel shades—but with a much shorter spike and the useful characteristic that it can be grown as a hardy annual—that is to say, plants will flower from seeds sown in the same year. This, too, has also been known to give flower in the third year which also makes it very nearly perennial. Biennial, buy seeds and sow as directed on the packet and in the introduction to this book.

DORONICUM—Leopard's Bane

The Doronicum or Leopard's Bane is one of the first perennials to flower. It will produce a mass of yellow daisies in April which, at that time, are very acceptable. Doronicum has a useful and unusual property—it will grow particularly well right on the roots of a Pyracantha. It is not a tall plant, seldom reaching more than 18in and, consequently, there is a point to be remembered in placing the Doronicum in the border—it is better right at the back of the border, for it will be in full flower long before many of the summer flowering perennials are so much as knee-high to a grasshopper. There are several varieties, although even the old Doronicum *plantagineum* gives a very good show for the little money it costs. 'Miss Mason' is a big yellow, and 'Spring Beauty' is double—if you like double flowers, although, personally, in this particular form, I don't. Buy plants from a nursery or garden centre and set them at any time in open weather from October to April. You can even plant them in flower.

ECHINOPS—Steel Globe Thistle

This might well be called a cultivated Thistle—and nothing could be easier than that. The name Steel Globe is appropriate because it has an icy blue flower which is long lasting in beauty. The leaves are covered in a downy fur giving them an added attraction. Many different varieties have been selected, and all are good. 'Taplow Blue' is tall, growing up to 5ft, 'Ritro' the type plant is also excellent. This is a valuable perennial which may be bought from a nursery or garden centre and—in my own experience—is better set in the spring, rather than in autumn.

ECHIUM

For some peculiar reason this plant, which matches the Nasturtium in more ways than one, is almost unknown. It grows just as easily, and the two together make a wonderful display right through from the end of June until the frosts come. It is a hardy annual which can be sown and grown without any difficulty. It also flowers at the same time as the Nasturtium, and the combination of the dwarf bedding varieties of that plant, which is the theme of this book (like 'Cherry Rose', 'Jewel Mixed' and 'Empress of India'), with the Echium called 'Blue Bedder' is a delight to the eye as much as it is a simple colour scheme to achieve. I sowed both of these together some ten years ago, in a particular patch of poor soil, and they have been coming up ever since to give me great pleasure for no effort at all. There are other forms of Echium which have been improved—if you can call it an improvement—by producing other colours, like pinks and mauves and purples—but I still believe that 'Blue Bedder' in company with—shall we say—the Nasturtium 'Cherry Belle' is one of the easiest and most decorative colour combinations that can be achieved in any garden, regardless of the skill or wealth of the owner.

ELAEAGNUS

There are many different varieties and species of this shrub. The one that is best known is called by various names—the most common of which, surprisingly, is Elaeagnus *pungens* 'Aurea Picta'. In this form it is an evergreen shrub with bright golden leaves that have a touch of green on the outside. It is the most colourful of all the variegated evergreen shrubs but it does have one big fault—it is all too easily inclined to revert to the pure green. Consequently, it is necessary to give it some slight attention by cutting out the green shoots as soon as they appear. Another variety is Elaeagnus *macrophylla*. It is not as spectacular as the variegated form but is none the less valuable for its silver-grey leaves and lily-of-the-valley type flowers which appear in October and are deliciously scented. Another similar hybrid, nowadays rather more plentiful, is Elaeagnus *ebbingei*. All these will reach a height of 8ft in ordinary garden soil. Buy pot grown or container grown plants from a nursery or garden centre and set them in the spring.

ELDER—see Sambucus

ELEPHANT'S EARS—see Bergenia

EPILOBIUM *angustifolium*

This is a weed—the Willow Herb which grows rampantly on commons and wild places, especially where there has been a fire. But what is a weed? It has been described as a plant in the wrong place. But the Willow Herb is seldom in the wrong place. It flowers in July with rosy-pink snapdragon blossoms which are followed by the light fluffy seedheads, almost as attractive as the flowers. It is true that it can become invasive and be a nuisance, but if you can control it—and even if you can't—it does have considerable decorative value from June right through to December. (Incidentally, it is a delight to flower arrangers.) You can obtain this by gathering plants from the common or picking the seed heads—or even by buying them from certain nurseries. There are some plant breeders who are paying particular attention to the Willow Herb to give it an even greater garden charm.

ERICA *carnea*—Alpine Heath—Winter Flowering Heather
Only the winter flowering heathers are included in this book because
the summer flowering varieties will only grow on a soil that does not
contain lime. The varieties of Erica *carnea*, the winter flowering
heather which is found on the Alps, is one of the best of all garden
plants. It brings colour into the garden from November to March and
the late varieties match up well with the Crocuses and early Daffodils.
There are many different sorts and all of them are good. The four that
are the most reliable are Erica *carnea* itself which has flesh pink buds
deepening to dark rose, almost red; Erica *carnea* 'King George', more
dwarf in habit with paler buds at the start but deeper colour at the
finish, towards the end of April; Erica 'Darleyensis' which has rosy-
pink flowers that start in November and have been known to go on
until May—a taller grower, up to 18in; and the two Springwoods,
Erica *carnea* 'Springwood', with long sprays of white flowers, and
Erica *carnea* 'Springwood Pink', similar in its spreading habit but with
flowers of a good clear pink. Erica 'Darleyensis' is a hybrid between
Erica *carnea* and Erica *mediterranea*. It is the longest flowering winter
heather. The lilac pink buds open in November and often go on until
May. All of these and other varieties of Erica *carnea* should be bought
as open ground plants or in pots and set at any time in open weather
from October to April

The tree heathers will also grow on any soil. These, incidentally,
are the plants from which briar pipes are made. The name comes from
the French word for heather, *bruyère*, and has nothing to do with roses.
The strongest tree heather of all is Erica *arborea* 'Alpina' which, like
the rest, makes a big bush up to about 8ft. It has two uses in the garden
—a fine display of white flowers in March, and these have the same
rather attractive coconut scent as the Common Gorse, and the foliage
and form are attractive enough for the shrub to do duty as a small
conifer when it is out of flower. There are other similar species and
hybrids like Erica *lusitanica* (The Portuguese Heath) and Erica 'Veitchii',
a hybrid with a faint pink tinge. But the best of all for flower is Erica
australis which gives a beautiful show of pink in March and April.
There are one or two discerning gardeners who think that these shrubs
even more beautiful when they are out of flower, for they then have
the appearance of small conifers and can do duty to provide this effect

THE PLANTS FOR PERFORMANCE

in any garden where space is limited. As with some other plants—like the Ceanothus and the Cistus—the tree heathers may be killed to the ground in a hard winter like that of 1963 but they will grow again quite satisfactorily from the root which remains unharmed. Buy plants, which must be pot grown, from a nursery or garden centre, and set them at any time in open weather from October to April.

The tree heathers need no attention but if the winter flowering heathers grow a little lanky, then they may be clipped over lightly with the shears as soon as they have finished flowering.

ESCALLONIA

If you live by the sea then the Escallonia is an evergreen, summer flowering shrub which can offer a great variety of different colours—in shades of white, pink and red—and different forms of growth and types of foliage. But inland the choice is more limited because some varieties are rather tender. Escallonias 'Langleyensis' and 'Edinensis' are two of the hardy varieties somewhat similar to each other. Both have strawberry pink flowers but Escallonia 'Langleyensis' is taller, reaching up to 9 or 10ft in time. Escallonia 'Donard Seedling' is a pale pink with light green foliage and is useful for hedgemaking, but a plant that is similar in general appearance, more compact in habit, growing to about 3½–4ft compared with 'Donard Seedling's' 8 or 9ft, is Escallonia 'Apple Blossom'. Like so many plants with this delightful name, its flowers are pink and white and very decorative. Buy young shrubs—grown in pots or containers—from a nursery or garden centre and set them at any time in open weather from October to April.

EUONYMUS—Spindle Tree

Spindle Tree is the name of the wild plant that grows in our hedgerows. It is not as plentiful as it was once, but when the bright orange balls are seen inside the red berries it is one of the delights of the countryside in autumn. There is a variety that has been selected called Euonymus *europaeus* 'Red Cascade' which has even larger berries in brighter colours. It may not be found in stock in every nursery or garden centre but it is well worth searching for. Euonymus *alatus* is a species from China and is one of the most brilliant of all autumn coloured shrubs. Not only that, but it has a singularly attractive habit of growth —angular, almost geometric—and the stems are covered with long 'fins', which make it a plant of some beauty in the winter. Another plant with the very long name of Euonymus *fortunei radicans* 'Variegatus' is useful in all sorts of odd positions—on the rock garden, as a ground cover plant, in the mixed border, as an edging and it can even be clipped into a low hedge, like Box. It is a creeping plant with silver and green variegated leaves which turn pink in the winter. Suitably placed, perhaps in conjunction with Cotton Lavender (Santolina *chamaecyparissus*) or other ground cover plants, it can provide a permanent feature of interest. All these may be bought as open ground plants or in containers. The two deciduous varieties—Euonymus *europaeus* and Euonymus *alatus*, may be set at any time in open weather from October to April, but the evergreen variety, Euonymus *japonicus radicans variegata*, is better planted in the spring.

EUPHORBIA—Spurge

The spurges are intriguing plants with a character all of their own— many of them look as though they might have been thought up by a writer of science fiction. Euphorbia *epithymoides* is one of the most decorative, yet rather underwritten in catalogues. It forms a neat clump of green, about 1ft high and 1ft across, and in the spring, just when the daffodils have finished flowering, it is covered in bright yellow flowers which, as they mature, are almost orange. It is useful for ground cover or for planting in a herbaceous or mixed border. Euphorbia *wulfenii* is a shrub with long waving stems of grey-green foliage and big heads of flowers throughout the spring. It is a distinctive plant, growing to about 4ft, and needs a special place in the garden— rather like Angelica. Another rather curious plant is the Caper Spurge— Euphorbia *lathyrus*. Unlike the other two, which are perennial, this is an annual or biennial. It grows into a very neat plant, about 3½ft high, with long stems which carry greenish yellow flowers that develop into round seedheads, like capers. The leaves are grey-green, long and pointed. It is said that this plant will keep moles away from a garden but this is not true. I have a small plantation and a colony of moles runs alongside it, almost among the roots. All of the three are decorative and they are particularly useful for flower arrangement, for they last well in water. Buy plants of Euphorbia *epithymoides* and Euphorbia *wulfenii* from a nursery or garden centre but it is necessary to grow Euphorbia *lathyrus* from seed which will only be obtainable from one of the specialist seed houses and is unlikely to be found on the racks in a seed store or garden shop.

FATSHEDERA

This hybrid between the Fatsia and the Ivy is a semi-climbing plant with dark green foliage, like an enlarged Ivy, and is very useful for planting in shaded places, particularly in town gardens, where it half grows, half climbs to about 5ft. Like the Ivy, it also makes an excellent houseplant. Buy plants from a nursery or garden centre, which must be grown in pots or containers, and set them in the spring.

FATSIA *sieboldii*

This is probably the most fascinating of all the hardy evergreen shrubs. It has enormous leaves, rather like those of a fig, and they are smooth and shiny so the Fatsia will grow quite happily in smoky districts. The flowers are equally intriguing, they are like enormous white antennae, and they appear in October, when there is little else in flower. This shrub is well worth growing for its foliage and form alone. Like the Camellia, the Fatsia spent many years inside the greenhouse because it was thought to be tender. It was used widely for indoor decoration in Victorian times and was discovered about the middle of the nineteenth century in Japan by Philip Frans von Siebold who sold it to the London nursery firm of Hendersons of St Johns Wood for £200, which was a great deal of money in those days. Depending on the soil and situation, it will grow up to about 7ft. Plants, preferably grown in pots or in containers, should be bought from a nursery or garden centre and set in the early autumn or in the spring.

FEBRUARY

Camellia, Cornus, Crocus, Erica, Galanthus, Galega, Hamamelis, Iris, Jasminum, Mahonia, Narcissus, Primula, Prunus, Sarcococca, Scilla, Viburnum.

FILIPENDULA—The Meadow Sweet

This is, quite literally, a cultivated weed. It grows wild in damp meadows and is as lovely there as it is in a border. There is one form that is an improvement, although it is double flowered and some people regard that as being a little artificial. Even so, Filipendula *ulmaria* 'Plena' produces a froth of creamy-white flowers up to a height of 3–4ft. There are some other varieties—like a beautiful golden form which is somewhat rare, but these are not so easy to grow. The Double Meadowsweet, which is the one I advise, is a perennial, so buy plants from a nursery or garden centre and set them in the spring.

FOLIAGE

Some species and varieties of the following plants are worth growing for their foliage alone: Angelica, Aucuba, Bergenia, Chamaecyparis, Cineraria, Cornus, Corylus, Elaeagnus, Euonymus, Fatshedera, Fatsia, Hebe, Hedera, Ilex, Mahonia, Melissa, Phillyrea, Prunus (Laurel), Rheum, Rhus, Rosemary, Rubus, Ruta, Salvia, Sambucus, Sedum, Senecio, Skimmia, Viburnum, Vitis, Weigela, Yucca.

FORGET-ME-NOT—see Myosotis

FORSYTHIA

This deciduous shrub gives the first big splash of yellow in the early spring. It is a positive joy because it comes out with so many flowers just at the moment when winter is over—it usually begins to give colour on the first day of spring, 21 March. Many different varieties have been raised from all the species that have been introduced over the years but there are only a few that are now worth planting. Forsythia 'Spectabilis' is an old-established form with big flowers in bright yellow. Forsythia 'Lynwood' is similar, but with rather larger individual flowers in a more attractive shade of yellow, less glaring, less blatant. Forsythia *suspensa* has long arching sprays which can be trained over a stake to form a semi-weeping bush or it can be grown on a trellis on the side of a house. The flowers are not so plentiful as on the other two, being wider spaced on the branches, but it does have its own particular charm and grace. If you want one that is even a little more attractive then it is worthwhile searching for Forsythia *suspensa atrocaulis*. This has the same habit of growth as Forsythia *suspensa* but the stems are dark brown, almost black, and these give a more dramatic effect to the pale yellow flowers. Forsythia 'Beatrix Farrand', raised in America, is of more bushy habit than the others, more compact and thick in growth and will, in time, reach 6 or 7ft although it is often classified as a dwarf. All these, or any of them, are worth planting in any garden but they do have one slight fault. After that first great glorious burst of flower is over they can be a little dull. You are then stuck with a very ordinary green bush remaining for the rest of the year—from April to November without so much as the attraction of autumn colour, bark, or habit of growth. The solution to this is to use the theme plant of this book. Plant near to your Forsythia some climbing varieties of the 'Golden Gleam' Nasturtium to ramble over it to give flower during the summer. The closer they are to the roots, the better they will flower. Forsythias can be obtained as open ground plants or as plants grown in containers from any good nursery or garden centre and they may be set at any time in open weather from the beginning of November until the beginning of March. You cannot expect any great show of flowers from those that are late planted. There is one small point of cultivation with this shrub that is worth remembering. The flowering stems should be cut back as soon as the flowers are over and it is worthwhile trimming round the bushes, or pinching back the long shoots in late July in order to encourage the formation of flower bud for the following year.

FOXGLOVE—see Digitalis

FUCHSIA

You will often hear stories of Fuchsia hedges in Ireland and in Cornwall —and these are rather inclined to give the impression that Fuchsias only grow in the open garden in those places. But the Fuchsia has a much wider use than this. It can be grown anywhere—provided you choose the right varieties. And there are many of these that are now well known to be perfectly hardy. They may not behave as the shrubs they are, but more like perennials, needing to be cut down every year in the spring. The best known of them all is Fuchsia 'Riccartonii' which gives a constant show of red flowers from late June right through to the autumn. Fuchsia *magellanica* is another, rather similar, but it also has a variety called 'Versicolor' which has the added attraction of leaves that are variegated pink, white and pale green. 'Mrs Popple' has larger flowers than most of the hardy varieties, in bright red and purple. 'Purple Splendour' is a good double red and purple with a spreading habit, and 'Madam Cornelissen' is scarlet and white. To my mind, the not so well known variety called 'Mrs W. P. Wood' is even more desirable. It has light green leaves and pale pink flowers, the whole creating a delightfully cool effect in August when it is at its best. These are only a few of the hardy varieties, for much work is being done to try out all sorts of Fuchsias all over the country to see just how many will stand being left outside all the year round. Others that can be relied upon, on present experience, are 'Brilliant', scarlet and purple; 'Cocconia floriana', blue and old rose; and 'Peggy King', red and blue. These all grow to about 3ft with the exception of Fuchsia 'Riccartonii' which will reach as much as 5ft in favourable conditions. The only attention they need is to cut down the old dead stems at the end of the winter. Buy pot grown plants from a nursery or garden centre and set them in the spring.

GAILLARDIA—Blanket Flower

Nobody is quite sure why this very decorative perennial (see page 51) is called the Blanket Flower, but it may be because it has the same brilliant colouring of yellow and dark maroon as the blankets of the Navajo Indians—and it comes from their country. It is one of the easiest of all perennials to grow—I even find that it seeds itself in gravel paths that have been treated with an all-out weedkiller. There are many different varieties but one of the most decorative is 'Mandarin', orange red with a dark centre, followed by 'Wirral Flame' which has deep red flowers and, if you want a lighter colour, 'Croftway Yellow' is a rich golden yellow with a bronze centre. All of these grow to about 3ft and are at their best in August. Buy plants from a nursery or garden centre and set them in the spring.

GALANTHUS—Snowdrop

The truth is that the Snowdrop is not a plant that will grow well absolutely everywhere—but as it is only difficult in very mild parts of the country, like Cornwall and the Scilly Isles, it seems fair to include it. There are big Snowdrops and bigger Snowdrops, and doubles and some that are green, almost yellow—and yet, in spite of all these, the old common plant, Galanthus *nivalis*, is still the best. If you do want to try one of the giants, then go for the sweetly scented G. *n.* 'S. Arnott'. If possible, Snowdrops should be planted as soon as they have finished flowering, which means buying British grown bulbs, but if only dried imported bulbs can be obtained, then plant at the beginning of September.

GALEGA—Goat's Rue

This is a very old perennial which is now not as well known as it should be. It more than qualifies for this book because, like the Nasturtium, it grows better in a poor soil than in one that is rich. It is—perhaps—a somewhat unkempt herbaceous perennial which grows to between 3 and 4ft and flowers from July and August. The flowers are pea shaped and plentiful. It has considerable value in giving light relief to a border at a time of year when strong colours are inclined to predominate. But, more than that, it makes a wonderful combination with the Spanish Broom and may be planted round it as a permanent support. The combination of the rich yellow of the Spanish Broom and the lilac colour of the Goat's Rue is delightful. There are several varieties but I recommend 'Her Majesty', a clear lilac to go with the Spanish Broom, or 'Lady Wilson' which is blue and white with rose shading. Buy plants from a nursery or garden centre and set them in the spring.

GARRYA *elliptica*

There is a singular charm in catkins—and especially when they are set off by dark-green evergreen foliage. Garrya *elliptica* is a plant which may be grown either as a shrub standing as a specimen, or against a wall trained on trellis work. It will reach as much as 10ft as a single specimen in good rich soil, and will climb up the side of the wall of a house with a little encouragement in the way of support and training. The long yellow catkins appear in the winter—January/February— when they are a positive joy. There is a curious story of coincidence about this plant. The shape of the catkins is exactly the same as the

'Swags' on the ornamentation of the Adams Brothers' mantelpieces and interior decorative work. In fact, the two are almost identical—yet the Garrya was not introduced into Europe for fifty years after the Adams brothers died. It is almost as if they had a pre-vision of this beautiful winter flowering evergreen shrub and used it in their designs. Buy pot or container grown plants from a nursery or garden centre and set them at any time in open weather from the end of October to April.

GENISTA *hispanica*—Spanish Gorse

This useful shrub forms round hummocks of prickly foliage about 1ft high and 2ft across which look as if they might have been trimmed into topiary specimens. In May and June it is covered with typical yellow, gorselike flowers. It can be grown in many places—on the rock garden, as an individual specimen beside a path or in a formal position for the benefit of its neat shape. It is said that this shape is the result of having been eaten for centuries by the goats in Spain which gave it the useful stunted appearance. Buy pot or container grown plants from a nursery or garden centre and set them in the early spring—March/ April.

GERANIUM—Cranesbills

The Geraniums should not be confused, in any way, with the Pelargonium, which is what most people know as the Geranium. The Pelargonium is a bedding out plant that is expensive, exotic, and needs careful cultivation and treatment if it is to last from year to year. But the hardy Geraniums are, for the most part, plants from our own wild hedgerows and meadows. It is difficult to overpraise them— they give flower over a long period and very decorative foliage that can be as attractive when it is old as when it is young. But these, like the British themselves, have been influenced and hybridised by foreign immigrants to give many plants that are of immense value in the garden. It is difficult to select the best but I would choose—for a start— two varieties, the progeny of a foreigner, Geranium *endressii*, which comes from the Pyrénées. One is called 'Wargrave Pink' and the other is 'Rose Claire'. These are both compact plants which reach 2ft high, at the most, and they are covered in flowers from June right through until the frosts become really severe. Both are pink, and a delightful shade at that. You could not ask for anything very much more because they need no attention, they will grow anywhere and give the same wonderful performance under any conditions. Then there are two blues that really are blue—the most delightful shade of that colour that can be imagined. Geranium *pratense* 'Plenum Coeruleum', an unfortunate name for such a simple plant, will reach as much as 3ft and it will give a mass of double flowers from June to August. In my own garden, I grow it with one of the Oenotheras, the 'Evening Primrose', and the two together are enough—so far as I am concerned—

Geranium 'Wargrave Pink'

for that period of the year when most gardens are swamped with garish bedding out plants. Geranium 'Johnsons Blue' or 'A. T. Johnson's Variety' is similar in its effect, but the flowers are single, and some may prefer these. It also has the advantage of a slightly lighter centre which gives an almost incandescent quality to the blossoms. One of the strongest, in terms of survival and constitution, is Geranium *sanguineum*—a slow growing, compact plant about 1ft high. This has rich magenta flowers in a striking shade of colour and it makes a splendid harmony with Centaurea *dealbata*, matching the base of the petals of this flower. Another good combination is with a light seedling Pink—for these two will grow together to form one clump. The soft lilac tones of the Pink blend well with the magenta and, even when there are no flowers, the silver-grey spears of the Pink foliage stand out in contrast above the dark-green, finely cut leaves of the Geranium. Buy plants from a nursery or garden centre, open ground or container grown, and set them in the spring.

GEUM

This well known plant is strictly a biennial—although it will behave as a perennial for a year or two. Even so, it is better to replace every two years at least. It is a good border plant, growing to a height of about 2½ft and producing a constant display of flowers—small rosettes of red or yellow. The red variety is called 'Mrs Bradshaw', and was found by chance in a garden in Southgate. The yellow variety is 'Lady Stratheden'. There are some newer sorts but they are not as good for their all-round performance as these two old stand-bys. Buy plants from a nursery or garden centre and set them in the early autumn.

GLADIOLUS

Gladiolus are difficult plants to place in a mixed flower garden. Their swordlike leaves and rather formal appearance are inclined to make them stand out too sharply from the other flowers. They are essentially flowers for exhibition and indoor decoration—but they do have their uses outside. Very often, at the end of May it is possible to see a small gap here and there which needs to be filled with something. This is the moment to plant two or three Gladiolus corms to give flower in

July—a month which can sometimes be a little drab. There are several different forms of this flower but the two that are best known are the large flowered, Grandiflora varieties and the smaller, Butterfly gladiolus. The best Grandiflora is 'Oscar', with a bright, large red flower which can be very effective against a tall mass of Michaelmas Daisy foliage. The best of the Butterflies is 'Green Woodpecker', a delightful mixture of cream and yellow with a spot of red in the centre and attractively crinkled petals. Strictly speaking, the Gladiolus is slightly out of the range of this book because it is not hardy. The corms need to be lifted in the autumn and stored for the winter. However, these varieties can be bought so cheaply nowadays that it is possible to take a risk and leave them in the ground—for they will often go on from year to year without harm, unless the winter is very hard. Buy corms and set them in May to a depth of about 4in.

GODETIA

This hardy annual, like Clarkia (see page 70), is another typical cottage garden flower. If it has a fault, it is that it grows too easily. The result is that a packet of seed can provide so many plants that they become overcrowded, unless thinning-out is done with ruthless determination. The modern answer to this is to buy pelleted seed and only sow twice as many as you think you will require, taking out the weakest when they are about 2in high. Godetias can be obtained in many different colours, and in packets of mixed seedlings. There are two principal types—the Azalea Flowered, which have a remarkable resemblance to the forced azaleas sold in florists shops at Christmas and Easter, and the tall double varieties, which grow to about 2ft and are particularly useful to provide cut flowers that last long. Buy seed, preferably pelleted, and sow in March and April.

GOLDEN ROD—see Solidago

GORSE—see Ulex

GRAPE HYACINTH—see Muscari

GROUND COVER

Low growing plants that will spread out to cover the ground and keep down the weeds. Not all the varieties listed under these names will do this, but some are excellent for the purpose. Alchemilla, Bergenia, Cistus, Cotoneaster, Erica, Euphorbia, Genista, Geranium, Hebe, Hedera, Heliantheum, Hypericum, Juniper, Lamium, Mahonia, Nepeta, Ruta, Santolina, Saxifraga, Sedum, Stachys, Vinca.

GYPSOPHILA

One of the very few plants that are known in the flower markets by their varietal names is Gypsophila 'Bristol Fairy'. For many years it was the traditional accompaniment to carnations and roses for table decoration and its dainty sprays of small white flowers are still used by modern flower arrangers. It is a delightful plant in a herbaceous or mixed border, giving a touch of lightness with its froth of white flowers which help to soften the harsher colours. It has the reputation of being a difficult plant to grow, but it is not. There is only one secret that must be known—the old foliage and flowers must be left to die down naturally on the plant, and never cut off while there is still a sign of life. There are other varieties—'Flamingo' is a slightly dwarfer pink form, and 'Rosy Veil' gives double flowers that start white and later turn pink. Buy plants from a nursery or garden centre and set them at any time in open weather from January to the end of March. Do not be put off by what appear to be dried old roots in polythene bags offered for sale in garden shops and garden centres. These are very strong plants which give an immediate show in the first year.

HAMAMELIS—Chinese Witch Hazel

There is nothing difficult about growing this fine winter flowering shrub in the garden—it is only expensive to buy because it is difficult to propagate. It will grow to a height of about 8 or 10ft, in time, and in the winter—usually about the middle to the end of January, it starts to produce its tiny starlike flowers, with a faint stripe of red at the base, and giving off one of the most delightful perfumes in the garden. It is a positive joy in the depth of winter, and a few sprigs of the flowers will scent a whole room. It is rather slow growing but it does

Lathyrus—
The Everlasting Pea, Lathyrus grandiflora, *will grow anywhere, even right on the roots of a Lime Tree. It has all the appearance of a Sweet Pea although it is a perennial and comes up every year. Only one thing is lacking—it has no scent*

Spartium *junceum*—
The 'Spanish Broom' (Spartium junceum) *is one of the brightest shrubs for late summer. It has a long flowering period and attractive rush-like stems in the winter*

Godetia—
Godetias are excellent hardy annuals for decoration in the garden and in the house. They are so easy to grow that thinning out unwanted seedlings is more of a problem than wondering whether they will come up

Mahonia *aquifolium*—
The 'Oregon Grape', Mahonia aquifolium, *is attractive in flower, berry and foliage. The leaves go purple in the winter and are useful for flower arranging*

flower at a very young stage and is perfectly hardy. There are some other varieties, but H. *mollis* is the best. Hamamelis *flavopurpurascens* as it should be called, but better known as H. *japonica rubra* is stronger growing, reaching 8ft in about five or six years, and the flowers are deeper in colour—but it has no scent. Plants from a nursery or garden centre must be container grown or have a solid ball of root held in a canvas wrap. Set them at any time in open weather from November to March.

HEATH—see Erica

HEBE

This is a new name for the shrubby Veronicas, to distinguish them from those that are herbaceous perennials. If you live by the sea there are countless varieties that you can grow in very attractive colours—including bright red and deep purple. But not all of these are hardy inland. Even so, there are many useful summer and autumn flowering dwarf evergreen shrubs among the hebes which can be grown with ease, anywhere. The best of all is probably Hebe 'Autumn Glory', a dwarf flowering shrub, reaching a height of about 18in, perhaps 2ft at times, with dark purply-green leaves and a fine display of rich purple flowers that start in June (in spite of its name) and go on until October. Another is Hebe 'Eversley Seedling', with narrow green leaves reaching a height of about 2 or 3ft. This has a mass of small flowers that are just off white, being a delightful shade of pale mauve pink. As with H. 'Autumn Glory' this variety will go on flowering until it is stopped by the frosts—it has been known to give a good show in December. Another that is useful for ground cover and as an evergreen is Hebe *sub-alpina*. This has light-green foliage and forms a round hummock of a plant about 12–18in high and 2 or even 3ft across. There are one or two more, and some of them are only curios, but Hebe *cupressoides* is a useful specimen plant for a small garden. Its foliage resembles that of a conifer and when the leaves are rubbed in the hand they give off an attractive aroma similar to that of a cedarwood pencil. Hebe *propinqua*, better known as H. *salicornoides*, is similar in the appearance of the individual leaf, but it is a dwarf plant, only about 6in high, and useful as an interesting form of ground cover. Buy plants, which must be

E   71

pot or container grown, from a nursery or garden centre and set them at any time in open weather from the end of October to the end of March.

HEDERA—Ivy

The Ivy has many uses—it can be planted as a ground cover plant where it has the useful trick of collecting the leaves that blow about the garden, it can even be used as a hedge and the tree forms make fine specimens with attractive flowers in October. Its best known use is as a climbing plant and nowadays it is frequently used for indoor decoration. There are many different forms and probably the best for the house or a sheltered position on a wall is the variety that is generally known as Hedera 'Gloire de Marengo', although its correct name is Hedera *canariensis variegata*. This has leaves which are deep green in the centre, then silvery-grey in the middle and edged with white—sometimes, for good value, there is a touch of pink. An iron-hardy variegated form is Hedera *colchica variegata*, with enormous leaves in yellow and green. An interesting new form is Hedera 'Gold Heart' which has much smaller leaves, set close together, and they have a rich golden yellow centre with a deep green border. The Tree Ivy is Hedera *helix arborescens* which makes a neat mound of evergreen foliage and carries the intriguing ivy flowers in October, and Hedera *helix tricolor* is another which has leaves of grey-green, white and rose pink. A climbing plant—buy container or pot grown from a nursery or garden centre and set at any time from October to the end of March.

HEDGING

Some species and varieties of the following plants are suitable for hedgemaking: Aucuba, Berberis, Chaenomeles, Chamaecyparis, Cotoneaster, Cupressocyparis, Erica, Escallonia, Forsythia, Hypericum, Ilex, Lavandula, Lavatera, Ligustrum, Lonicera, Mahonia, Prunus, Pyracantha, Rosemarinus, Tamarix, Ulex.

HELENIUM—Sneeze Weed

This strong growing perennial plant from North America is so tough that, along with Golden Rod and some of the Michaelmas Daisies, it always survives in a garden which has been completely neglected for some years. This is one of its troubles—it is so strong growing that the taller varieties become lank and need staking. However, there are others which are not quite so vigorous and will stay upright with little more than the support of a few pea sticks. Helenium 'Moerheim Beauty', with bronze red daisies, growing to about 3ft is one of the best known of all and still a good garden plant, as is 'The Bishop', about the same height, giving big yellow flowers. Helenium 'Gartensonne' is taller, but it is worth a little more trouble in keeping it upright in windy weather because of its large yellow flowers. Helenium 'Crimson Beauty', in crimson and gold, is shorter at 2ft and needs very little support. All flower from July to September—perennial—buy plants from a nursery or garden centre and set them in the spring.

HELIANTHEMUM—Sun Rose

There is a Sun Rose which is native to the British Isles but the cultivated varieties have been improved out of all recognition by the infusion of foreign blood. They are all dwarf shrubs, reaching about 12 to 15in in height and spreading to about 2ft. They have green or silver-grey foliage and produce a mass of flowers—in the mornings only—from June right through to August. They grow well in the poorest soil but they must have a sunny position. They are very easily grown from seed with the result that many varieties have been named and introduced. The best of all is one of the oldest called 'The Bride' which has creamy-white flowers with a yellow centre. The Royal Horticultural Society has tried out most of the best and their choice is indicated by those that have received the Award of Garden Merit 'for plants of proved and outstanding excellence for general garden work'. These are—'Amy Baring', deep yellow; 'Ben Fhada', yellow with orange centre, grey foliage; 'Ben Hope' carmine with orange centre, grey-green foliage; 'Jubilee', double primrose yellow; 'Mrs C. W. Earle', scarlet with a yellow flush, double; 'Watergate Rose', rose-crimson with orange centre, grey-green foliage; and 'Wisley Primrose', primrose yellow with deeper centre, grey-green foliage. Buy pot grown plants from a nursery or garden centre and set them in the spring, for preference.

HELIANTHUS—Sun Flower

Sun Flowers can either be perennial or annual. The perennial varieties are easily grown in herbaceous or mixed borders and two of the best of several varieties, which give flowers from July to September, are 'Soleil d'Or' (the same name as the well known narcissus), yellow with curved and pointed petals, growing to 4ft, and 'Loddon Gold', 5ft high, a rich double yellow. There is an excellent annual form called 'Sun Burst', which is a good flower for cutting, and, of course, there is the old giant Sun Flower which, in the right place, can be extremely effective.

The 'Jerusalem Artichoke' has nothing to do with Jerusalem, neither is it an artichoke—furthermore, it is normally grown as a vegetable, and yet it is a Sun Flower—Helianthus *tuberosus*. It is included because it makes an excellent quick screen—very useful in a new garden until something more permanent can be established. The thick stems, which can be cut and dried to use as flower stakes, grow quickly to 6 or 8ft—and it is said to clean the ground even better than potatoes. The tubers can be dug from October to February, scraped and cooked in water with a little vinegar, or made into a purée—very useful as a substitute for potatoes for slimmers, because they contain inulin instead of starch. Perennial. Plant tubers in December.

HEMEROCALLIS—Daylily

One of the oldest of all perennials grown in this country, the Daylily (see page 52) is so old, in fact, that no one now knows where it first came from. There was a time, until quite recently, when the only colours available were yellow, with no greater variety than pale yellow, deep yellow or near-orange. But since the end of World War II, the Americans have been hard at work breeding Hemerocallis and now you may have almost any colour—even a mauve. Daylilies have become something of a cult—and it is possible to pay a lot of money for some of the newer varieties. However, there are many excellent sorts that give a delightful show for no trouble at all—'Garnet Robe', a large velvety red; 'Ophir', large deep yellow; 'Pink Damask', deep coppery pink; 'Red Torch', dusky orange-red; 'Royal Ruby', cardinal red; and 'Salmon Sheen', pale salmon. Incidentally, do not be put off by the name Daylily. This only refers to individual flowers which come out and fade in a day, but there are so many of them that the Daylilies are a constant show of colour throughout July and August. Buy plants from a nursery or garden centre and set them at any time in open weather from October to April—they are almost indestructible.

HIBISCUS

Hibiscus *syriacus* has been grown in our gardens for nearly 400 years—so long, that nobody is certain where it came from originally, but it is doubtful if it was Syria. It is an easy going and hardy plant which produces crop after crop of flowers from July right through to September. It is so easy to grow that it has been used to plant up the centre of the Cromwell Road extension, one of the western routes out of London. It is a deciduous shrub which will grow up to 8 or 10ft, depending on the soil—in average gardens it usually reaches about 6 or 7ft. Many different varieties have been raised, mostly in France, but five of the best of those that are available today arc 'Woodbridge', a big pink; 'Hamabo', a single pink with a dark spot; 'Celeste' and a double form of the same variety, both blue; 'Bluebird', a single blue with a dark blotch at the base of the petal; and 'William R. Smith', a large single white with attractively crinkled flowers. There is one small warning about this shrub—it may hang fire for a year when it is first planted. That is to say, it will not throw either flowers or leaves or growth. But do not despair—leave it where it is and it will grow away quite happily in the following spring. Buy open ground plants or plants grown in containers from a nursery or garden centre and set them at any time in open weather from November to March.

HOLLY—see Ilex

HONEYSUCKLE—see Lonicera

HYDRANGEA

The well known Hortensia Hydrangeas are excluded from this book although they are said to be perfectly hardy. This is true of most gardens in the British Isles—but not all, including mine. Consequently, I would not recommend these beautiful shrubs for every garden.

However, there is one that is hardy everywhere and no less beautiful than those big balls of pink and blue. The variety is called Hydrangea *paniculata grandiflora*. It starts to flower towards the end of June when it puts out greenish buds which open to green-yellow young flowers, gradually turning to creamy white. As they mature, they take on a pink tinge until, at last, they finally fade. This Hydrangea needs to be pruned in exactly the same way as a hybrid tea rose, by cutting back the old growth in the spring to the second or third bud. It will then reach about 3 or 4ft in the summer. The other really hardy Hydrangea, which actually enjoys being grown on a north wall, is the climbing form called H. *petiolaris*. This is a self-clinging climber which will make its own way up a wall and give small, white hydrangea type flowers throughout the late summer. It is also very useful for covering an old tree trunk or any mound of earth which may be inconveniently placed, but difficult to move. The hardy Hydrangea *paniculata grandi-flora* is usually sold as an open ground plant and you can buy it in this way from a nursery or in a container from a garden centre. The climbing Hydrangea must always be bought as a pot grown or container grown plant. Both may be set at any time in open weather from the end of October to the end of March.

HYPERICUM—St John's Wort

Strictly speaking, the shrubby Hypericums, which are the best garden plants are not the 'St John's Wort'—this is a small annual, a weed. Probably one of the finest of all garden plants, to give flower in the late summer, is the shrub Hypericum 'Hidcote Variety'. It grows to about 3 or 4ft and from the end of June right through until the frost comes, it carries yellow flowers, like large buttercups, with glistening petals. It looks particularly well when it is planted near to Ceanothus 'Gloire de Versailles'. Another very good variety is Hypericum *patulum* 'Elstead Variety'. This has the distinction of carrying its flowers and red berries at the same time, doubling up on its charm. Then there is Hypericum 'Androsaemum', a very old plant known as Tutsan because it was thought to be a cure-all and was used by the early pharmacists for all sorts of different ailments. It is still used in one particular ointment and this was the only treatment that would relieve the pain of a friend of mine who lost a leg in the Blitz. Apart from its old time medicinal value, the black berries are singularly useful to the flower arranger to give a different colour in a different form. Hypericum 'Moserianum' just scrapes into this book because it might be considered fractionally tender. The fraction is so small that it would be wrong not to mention the neat shrub, growing to about 12 or 18in high and about 2ft across which, like Hypericum 'Hidcote', keeps on flowering all through the late summer with large yellow buttercups, made even more attractive by outstanding, starlike stamens. The maid-of-all-work among the Hypericums is H. *calycinum*. This is a strong growing ground cover plant which would soon cover a bank or spare piece of ground so effectively that there is no hope of any weed growing. The flowers are rather like those of Hypericum 'Moserianum' —the stamens stand up above the petals—but, somehow or other, it lacks this plant's singular charm, yet it does have a use because of its strong growth and extreme hardiness. Buy plants either open ground or container grown from a nursery or garden centre and set them in the spring.

ICELAND POPPY—see Papaver *nudicaule*

ILEX— Holly

The Holly is one of the five evergreen trees that are native to the British Isles. It is better known for its berries at Christmas time than for decoration in the garden. But an ordinary common Holly is far too big a tree to grow in the average garden today—and even then, you cannot be sure that it will berry because some are male, some female and some are bisexual. This difficulty can be overcome, for there is one variety that will berry freely, year in year out all on its own. This is called Ilex *altaclarensis* 'J. C. Van Thol'. It makes a tall, rather pyramidal bush, and it has dark leaves without many spines— another advantage if you are going to use it to stick in the Christmas pudding. It is a valuable addition to winter colour in the garden, without taking up very much room. So, too, are some of the variegated hollies of which the best are 'Golden King' and 'Silver Queen'. These were named without reference to their sex—for 'Golden King' is a female holly and bears berries, while 'Silver Queen' is male and can only be considered for the beauty of its leaves. Ilex 'Golden King' is one of the brightest variegated plants in the garden. Not only are the leaves well splashed with gold but, very often, the young growth is pure gold. Ilex 'Silver Queen' has leaves which are green, mottled with grey, and edged with silver. These are set off very attractively by the red stems of the young growth. Another variety, which is somewhat similar in the pattern of its leaves—but gold instead of silver—is Ilex *aquifolium* 'Madame Briot'. This has purple stems which, again, add to its charm. If you want berries and a somewhat bizarre type of growth, Ilex *aquifolium* 'Pendula' is a weeping form which makes an elegant bush and produces its berries all on its own, in the same way as I. 'J. C. Van Thol'. Buy plants from a nursery or garden centre and, believe it or not, the best time to set them is June.

INULA *magnifica*

This is a flamboyant perennial growing up to 5ft. The flowers are big yellow daisies, with long curly petals, but it is equally attractive as a foliage plant for it has green leaves about the size of a pointed shovel. It is so easy to grow that it seeds itself everywhere and will grow equally well in any type of soil although, I find, in my own garden that it naturalises more freely around the foundations of the house than anywhere else. It makes a big coarse root and is almost impossible to kill. The leaves, by the way, are of considerable use for floral arrangement. Perennial. Buy plants from a nursery or garden centre and set them in the autumn or the spring.

IRIS—Fleur-de-lis

What are known as the Tall Bearded Iris or the German Iris are some of the easiest of all plants to grow. In fact, it would not be going too far to say that they are difficult to kill. But the Iris has come a long way from the clump of old purples outside the back door. The range of colour available now is dazzling—almost any shade or combination of shades and tones and separate colours that you may wish. Like the Daylilies (Hemerocallis), this is largely due to the influence of American breeders who have produced some excellent varieties—although we have not been far behind, in spite of greater limitations of climate. But when it comes to performance in the garden, it is wiser not to choose those that live up to part of the name by being very tall—5ft or more. You will not be certain of positive success with these unless you are prepared to stake the spikes individually—which is boring. Again, like the Daylilies you can pay a lot of money for the best—but there are many available at a reasonable price—and a reasonable height. They all flower in June when their orchidlike shape makes a pleasant change from the other perennials out at that time. There are three points of beauty in the flowers of these Irises—the standards, the petals that stand upright; the falls, those that droop down; and the beard which is carried on the falls and links up with the standard petals. The following is a short list of those that are not too expensive—and not too tall. Height of each is given in brackets:

'Cliffs of Dover' (42in), still the best white flowered bearded Iris.

'Cloth of Gold' (36in), a deep yellow with orange beard and falls that flare outwards.

'Dancer's Veil' (36in), the British raised Iris which won all possible international awards in 1963—blue and purple on a white background.

'Elleray' (40in), soft yellow with a white flare—its perfect branching habit gives it stability.

'Headlines' (36in), standards blue paling to white, falls dark purple giving a dramatic contrast in colour.

'Native Dancer' (36in), peach pink with an orange beard and semi-flaring falls. A little more expensive than the others—but worth it.

'Party Dress' (34in), perhaps one of the best named flowers of all—flamingo pink petals which look as if they had been crimped with a gophering iron. About the same cost as 'Native Dancer', but this is one you must have.

'Patterdale' (40in), the palest of pale blues and with a branching habit that gives balance to the height.

'Sable Night' (36in), the darkest purple with a claret undertone and a dark brown beard—sounds menacing but is very effective.

'Staten Island' (38in), one of the best of the Americans—gold standards, rich red falls, and a strong grower.

'Tarn Hows' (34in), a curiously well named plant—dark brown, almost mahogany, as the sound of the name implies.

Intermediate Bearded Irises: Because of the problem of height, and damage by wind and rain, a new type of bearded Iris has been raised in recent years called Intermediate. These flower rather earlier than the others—during the last two weeks in May—and they are shorter in growth, ranging from 15in to 2ft. Many different varieties have been raised by amateur growers, but it is some time before these will be on the market. However, in the meantime, there are four which can be obtained and are well worth growing, both for their garden decoration, and to extend the Iris season with plants that need no support. 'Chiltern Gold' is golden yellow, 2ft; 'Lime Grove', white standards and flaring greenish-yellow falls edged with white, 16in; 'Little Cottage' is a flaring white self to 16in; and 'Scintilla' has ivory standards above golden falls and grows to 20in.

Dwarf Bearded Iris: There is yet another race which has been produced by crossing the tall bearded Irises with the very dwarf species. These all grow to about 1ft and may either double up as front plants for the herbaceous border or grow on their own in the rock garden. A short selection is: 'Austrian Sky', a sky-blue self with a darker mark on the fall; 'Bright Eyes', lemon yellow with a blue mark on the fall; 'Little Rosy Wings', a rosy red, rather shorter than the rest; 'Pigmy Gold', a brilliant yellow which is scented; and 'Tinkerbell', lobelia blue with a deeper flush.

Iris sibirica: The Irises that come from Siberia are different. They are tall growing and they have no beards. They are very easy to grow and flower in June and July. One of the oldest of all is called 'Caesar' growing to a height of about 4ft, with dark-purple flowers. Nowadays there are other varieties like 'Camberley', a clear blue up to 3ft; 'Helen Astor', which is a reddish pink and useful to set off the blue varieties; and 'Snow Queen', a clear white growing to 3ft.

Iris Species: Perhaps the most exciting of all the Irises is the species that is now called by the curious name of Iris *unguicularis*, although it is still better known by its old name of *stylosa*. This is the winter flowering Iris. It will grow well in any poor soil—the poorer the better—in any exposed position, although somewhere with shelter from the north-east will produce flowers earlier. It grows to about 1ft and, according to the season, it will throw its pale blue flowers, which are as delightful to see in the garden as they are to use for cutting for the house, from November to March.

Iris pseudo-acorus: This should not be left out because it is our own native Iris. It is the yellow Flag, and it ought to be omitted because it does prefer a damp situation. Even so, it is a plant that grows in many parts of the world and it has one curious characteristic—it never varies. Many other plants produce different forms, in different colours, or different shapes, but the good old Flag is always the same—a tall spike of yellow flowers in classic Iris shape.

Buy plants from a nursery or garden centre and set them in July or August, although the I. *sibiricas* may be planted in the spring.

ISATIS *tinctoria*—Woad

This biennial should be in every British garden. It is a very decorative plant growing to about 3ft, giving a froth of small yellow flowers in June, rather like those of the Gypsophila, followed by shiny black seeds that are equally attractive. It is also the source of the dye, woad, which some people say gave the name to Britain. The Celtic word for stained was *brithon*. So, when the Celts came to the British Isles, a Brithon was a stained man, a native of the country. The plant, incidentally, like the Ancient Britons, is a little unruly but this is no fault. Its somewhat wild and woolly appearance makes a pleasant change from the strict spikes of Lupins and Delphiniums which are inclined to dominate the border in June. Isatis *tinctoria* may be a little difficult to obtain nowadays—but it is well worth some effort. If possible, buy plants from a nursery and save the seeds or obtain some seed from a specialist seedsman and grow it yourself in the same way as other biennials.

JANUARY

Some species and varieties of the following plants flower in January: Camellia, Chaenomeles, Crocus, Erica, Galanthus, Garrya, Hamamelis, Iris, Jasminum, Lonicera, Mahonia, Prunus, Viburnum.

JAPANESE CHERRY—see Prunus

JASMINE—see Jasminum

JASMINUM—the Jasmine or Jessamine

The summer flowering Jasmine—Jasminum *officinale grandiflora*—is as much a part of the cottage as the Hollyhock is of the garden in front of it. Yet it is not a natural climbing plant and needs to be trained with the help of wires or trellis work. Throughout the summer it carries its white flowers with their distinctive and delicious perfume. It is a very strong grower, and needs to be pruned back after it has flowered and the branches thinned out, otherwise it becomes tangled up with dead growth. It has been grown here for so long that it has almost come to be regarded as a native plant—like Lilac and Lavender. But perhaps the winter flowering Jasmine, Jasminum *nudiflorum*, which has only been with us since the middle of the nineteenth century, is even more useful. It is still less of a natural climber than Jasminum *officinale grandiflora* but, probably because of the tradition formed by the summer flowering plant, it is nearly always grown on a wall or fence. However, it makes an excellent bush, in its own right, if it is given a little support in the form of a tripod and allowed to ramble over this. It gives a constant show of yellow flowers from December right through to February but, unfortunately, without scent. Jasminum *nudiflorum* should be cut back when it has finished flowering and the branches thinned out. A good combination is to grow it behind some shrubs of Mahonia *aquifolium* in order to enjoy the contrast between its yellow flowers and the dark purple leaves of the mahonia. Buy plants, which must be pot or container grown, from a nursery or garden centre and set them at any time from October to the end of March.

JULY

Some species and varieties of the following plants flower in July: Alchemilla, Begonia, Buddleia, Calendula, Campanula, Caryopteris, Ceanothus, Centaurea, Ceratostigma, Cistus, Clarkia, Coreopsis, Digitalis, Delphinium, Dianthus, Echinops, Echium, Epilobium, Escallonia, Filipendula, Fuchsia, Gaillardia, Galega, Geranium, Geum, Gladiolus, Godetia, Gypsophila, Hebe, Helianthemum, Hibiscus, Lonicera, Hydrangea, Hypericum, Inula, Lathyrus, Lavatera, Lavender, Leycesteria, Ligularia, Lilium, Lobularia, Lonicera, Lychnis, Macleaya, Melissa, Monarda, Nepeta, Oenothera, Perowskia, Petunia, Phlox, Phygelius, Physalis, Physostegia, Polygonum, Ranunculus, Rhus,

Rose, Rudbeckia, Ruta, Santolina, Scabiosa, Sedum, Senecio, Solidago, Spartium, Spiraea, Stachys, Tamarix, Tropaeolum, Verbascum, Vinca, Yucca.

JUNE

Some species and varieties of the following plants flower in June: Alchemilla, Campanula, Catananche, Ceanothus, Centaurea, Clarkia, Clematis, Cytisus, Dianthus, Digitalis, Delphinium, Echium, Escallonia, Geranium, Geum, Godetia, Gypsophila, Helianthemum, Hypericum, Jasminum, Laburnum, Lathyrus, Lavatera, Lilium, Lobularia, Lonicera, Lupinus, Macleaya, Monarda, Nepeta, Oenothera, Origanum, Paeonia, Papaver, Petunia, Philadelphus, Phlox, Polygonatum, Potentilla, Ranunculus, Rhus, Rose, Salvia, Scabiosa, Spiraea, Verbascum.

JUNIPER—see Juniperus

JUNIPERUS—Juniper
One of our few native evergreens—the common Juniper, Juniperus *communis*, was dearly loved by Gertrude Jekyll but its ungainly growth and bronzy-green colouring does not fit in easily with the gardens of today. Even so, there are many junipers that are still useful and the variety of the common Juniper called Juniperus *communis compressa* is a perfect plant for the rock or sink garden. Even when it is very old it will seldom grow more than 4 or 5ft—and that takes thirty years or more. It forms a slim narrow column, making a perfect miniature tree. Juniperus *sabina tamariscifolia*, the Spanish Juniper, is an excellent spreading plant which can be used either for ground cover in the front of a shrub or mixed border or as a specimen at the end of a terrace or wall. It seldom grows taller than 1ft but spreads out as much as 8ft. When it has its young growth during the summer it is light grey-green in colouring and looks as if it is constantly smothered in dew. Juniperus *pfitzeriana* is a taller plant which grows in layers. It might well be described as typically Japanese in outline and form. It will reach as high as 6 or 7ft when it will be 8 or 10ft through. But this takes a long time. Juniperus 'Blaauwii' is a new variety with rather more angular growth, and branches coming out at about 45°, carrying leaves that are

an intriguing shade of metallic blue. The latest addition to the ornamental Junipers is Juniperus *virginiana* 'Sky Rocket', a slim conifer which grows fast—ideal as a single specimen in a small garden. Juniperus *virginiana*, incidentally, is the pencil cedar with the wood that has that delightful distinct aromatic scent. Buy plants, either open ground or container grown, from a nursery or garden centre and set them in the early autumn or in the spring.

KERRIA—Jews Mallow

The double flowered form of this shrub—Kerria *japonica fl. pl.* (see page 52)—was introduced to this country early in the nineteenth century and it became so popular that within 35 years it was to be found growing almost everywhere, even in the smallest cottage gardens. It has long green stems, reaching up to 8ft, and green leaves. It carries double yellow flowers in April and May, but even when these are over, the shrub is still attractive for the bright green of its twigs and foliage, which are also useful for flower decoration. Buy plants, either open ground or in containers, from a nursery or garden centre and set them at any time from the end of October to the end of March.

LABURNUM—Golden Rain

There are Laburnums and Laburnums—and the old common variety, Laburnum *vulgare*, is not worth planting nowadays. Laburnum 'Vossii', for example, has racemes of yellow flowers in May, which are at least twice as long as those of the other species. Laburnum 'Watererii' is another with long flowers and is later to flower—going well on into June. These trees are excellent for small gardens, to give flower and shade, but it should be remembered that the seeds can be poisonous to children who must be warned not to touch them. Buy bushes or standard trees, open ground or container grown, from a nursery or garden centre and set them at any time in open weather from the end of November to the end of March.

LAMIUM—Dead Nettle

You cannot have a better plant for performance, so far as growth is concerned, than a cultivated weed—always provided it gives a good performance either in foliage or in flower. Lamium *maculatum*, the variegated form of the Dead Nettle qualifies under all headings. It is as easy to grow as the weed itself. The leaves of the plant are dark green striped with white. It carries successive crops of mauve flowers throughout the year and these act as an excellent foil to others—particularly as the plant is low growing and creeping, ideal for edging and the front of any border. Buy plants from a nursery or garden centre and set them at any time in open weather from the end of October to the end of March.

LARKSPUR—see Delphinium

LATHYRUS *odoratum*—Sweet Pea

There is probably no more difficult plant to grow for exhibition than the Sweet Pea (Lathyrus *odoratum*). And there is probably no easier plant to grow in the garden for decoration, over a long period, than the sweet pea. There is no need to trench the ground 4ft deep and run the flowers up on single stems to achieve the maximum size and perfection. Sweet peas may be sown outdoors to ramble over any eyesore, like a tree trunk—and they are particularly useful for climbing up through winter and early spring flowering shrubs to give colour during the summer. The method is very simple indeed, as it relies on one of the few firm dates in the gardeners' calendar. Seeds should be sown outdoors on 10 October—or as near to it as possible. Seeds can also be sown in this way to grow plants on rough tripods of bean sticks to have a clump of sweet peas in a mixed border. The most showy kinds are the Spencers which can be bought as mixed seedlings, but if you wish to choose your colours the following is a selection: white—'Swan Lake'; scarlet—'Airwarden'; cerise—'Percy Izzard'; carmine—'Carlotta'; mauve—'Leamington'; pink—'Piccadilly'; pink and yellow—'Frolic'. These are the classic varieties, and there is a new strain called Galaxy with larger flowers and more of them but they are only available as mixed seedlings. Buy seeds from a seedsman—and sow on 10 October.

Lathyrus *grandiflora*, the Everlasting Pea (see page 69), is almost indestructible. I have some plants growing in a meadow which are only there because they were thrown on a bonfire. In appearance, it is exactly like a Sweet Pea, and although the flowers last only for a day so many of them keep coming that you do not notice this ephemeral quality. The leaves, too, are rather like those of a Sweet Pea and were it not for one sad fact, the two would be identical—it has no scent. Even so, it is a valuable plant to grow in a mixed border or left to wander in its own rampant way. Incidentally, one of the places where it will grow is where nothing else can hope to survive—right on the roots of a Lime tree. Buy plants from a nursery or garden centre and set them at any time in open weather from October to March.

LAUREL—see Prunus

LAVANDULA—Lavender

Old English Lavender, Lavandula *spica*, is one of our oldest garden shrubs—but it is not English. It came originally from the region of the Mediterranean—but it came so long ago that it is now regarded as a basic plant of the English garden. Lavandula *spica* is, undoubtedly, the best for scent. Both the flowers and the leaves give off the comforting perfume associated with clean linen kept in oak chests. There are many other Lavenders: 'Munstead Variety' is associated with that great English gardener, Miss Gertrude Jekyll, it is more dwarf than the Old English, darker in colour but, perhaps, with not quite so strong a scent. 'Twickel Purple' is the darkest of all and Lavandula *vera*, known as Dutch Lavender, is neat and compact and silver-grey in foliage but with only half the scent of Old English. Like all grey-foliaged plants, lavender should only be planted in the spring. Buy from a nursery or garden centre, either open ground or container grown—but it is not worth paying the extra money for container plants. When the shrubs are established, cut them back hard, every year, at the beginning of April.

LAVATERA—Mallow

There are two kinds of mallow, widely different in character. The Tree Mallow is a shrub which will grow to about 6 or 7ft and produce a constant succession of rose-pink flowers, rather like single holly-hocks, on grey stems covered with grey leaves, during the summer. This is called Lavatera *olbia rosea*. There is also an annual form which is equally attractive, if not more so—so far as the flowers are concerned.

Lunaria—
'Honesty' (Lunaria) is one of the oldest cultivated plants and may even be a native. Its mauve flowers come out with the daffodils and its big white seed heads in the winter look like fairies dancing for joy

Polyanthus—
The polyanthus is correctly called a primula and is a hybrid between the cowslip and the primrose. Its long flowering period and wide range of colour makes it invaluable in the garden. Can also be used as a pot plant for decoration in the house

Rose 'Peace'—
The Hybrid Tea Rose 'Peace' was one of the sensations of the post war period. Its big creamy flowers, just touched with pink, are held on strong stems clothed with lustrous green leaves

The best known is Lavatera 'Loveliness', a hardy annual which will grow to about 2 or 3ft and produce a display of flowers, larger and more colourful than the Tree Mallow, from July right through to the frosts. But it has to be sown every year. Buy plants of the Tree Mallow from a nursery or garden centre, preferably pot or container grown, and set them in the spring. Treat the annual mallow, Lavatera 'Loveliness' as a hardy annual.

LAVENDER—see Lavandula

LEYCESTERIA

The common name of Leycesteria *formosa* is Elisha's Tears. This is not so much an indication of the drooping habit of the flowers and bracts as it is the result of the pronunciation and adaptation of the Latin name. If you pronounce 'ley' as 'lie' and add an 'h' in after the 'c', you have something which sounds vaguely like—Elisha's Tears. But, whatever the name, this is a shrub of considerable value. It grows with long green stems, rather like those of a bamboo, and they produce white flowers which are held by red bracts in the late summer and early autumn. They then develop into reddish-purple berries, like small gooseberries in October. It grows to about 4 or 5ft in a season and should be cut back hard in the spring in order to enjoy the benefit of the fresh green stems which are no small part of its charm. Buy plants from a nursery or garden centre, they may either be open ground or container grown, and set them in the spring.

LIGULARIA *clivorum*

There is no common name for this plant but it is closely related to the common groundsel. It is as useful for its foliage, large heart-shaped leaves on stalks about 1ft high as it is for its bright orange daisies in July and August. It is a perennial which is easy to grow with, perhaps, a preference for a shady place. Buy plants from a nursery or garden centre, although they may be rather hard to find, and set them in the spring.

LIGUSTRUM—Privet

This shrub may seem to be outdated, almost too common to mention.

And there is no doubt that the Oval Leaved Privet, Ligustrum *ovalifolium*, the widely grown hedge plant, is something of a danger in the modern garden, where space is limited, because it is so greedy. It needs at least 4ft for its root run before anything else can be planted with any hope of success. The Golden Privet, Ligustrum *ovalifolium aureum*, is another matter. It is a brightly variegated evergreen plant which will give colour all the year round and adds something to a mixed border which can help to fill any awkward gap when there are no flowers in bloom. Ligustrum *tricolor* is even more attractive but just a little tender. Still, it is worth a try for its leaves which are silver, green and, when young, pink. The Common Privet, Ligustrum *vulgare*, should not be despised. It is a native plant, and semi-evergreen, but its chief attraction is in its black berries—highly prized by flower arrangers.

LILAC—see Syringa

LILIUM—Lily

Lilies were considered to be very difficult plants indeed. They were either grown in greenhouses for indoor decoration or, when they were grown outside, they needed all kinds of different treatment— some preferred chalk, others wanted an acid soil, some had to be planted deep, some shallow—and so on. But all that is changed. There are now several different hybrid races of lilies which can be planted in any soil at roughly 2½ times their own depth. Yet, there is still one lily with a peculiar preference of its own which, I feel, should be included in this book for that very reason. This is Lilium *candidum*, the 'Madonna' Lily, one of the oldest cultivated ornamental plants in the world. The peculiarity about the Madonna Lily, which is generally recognised but impossible to prove by any form of scientific investigation is that it grows best in small gardens. It seems to like the close confines of hedges or fences, but if it is planted where there are spacious lawns and gracious cedars, it seems to languish and die. Another lily, which is not so old in cultivation but will grow almost anywhere, is Lilium *regale*. This is as beautiful as it is easy to grow. It is a white trumpet lily with a golden throat and the outsides of the petals are shaded with deep maroon—and it is beautifully scented.

Lilium 'Enchantment'

Among the modern hybrids the Mid-Century group offer some of the best—and the best of the best is, undoubtedly, Lilium 'Enchantment'. This is a lily which grows to about 2 or 3ft and flowers in July with big trumpets that are held upright in the most brilliant orange imaginable. Not only that, it grows so freely that it is almost as prolific as a Michaelmas Daisy. There are many other named varieties—'Destiny' is a good yellow and so, too, is 'Golden Chalice', and there is a new dark red called 'Ruby' which is equally prolific. The bulbs of the Mid-Century hybrids may also be bought as mixed seedlings which are good—and cheap. Then there are the Fiesta hybrids with long sprays, up to 5ft, of hanging flowers in Turk's cap form and the Olympic hybrids, mostly in shades of fuchsia pink in trumpet lily form. The Bellingham hybrids are mostly dark orange with deep red, nearly black, spots, again in Turk's cap shape—and the many new hybrids of Lilium *auratum*, the Golden Rayed Lily of Japan, are the most spectacular of all. Some of the easiest to grow, with their great big trumpet flowers, are 'Empress of China', a pure white with tiny purple dots, 'Empress of India', deep red with a narrow white rim, and 'Empress of Japan' which, like the original, is white with golden rays.

For the best results with these modern garden lilies it is preferable to obtain them as British grown bulbs and plant them in the early autumn—but, unfortunately, there are not many British lily growers. However, I have had excellent success myself by planting in January from imported bulbs, which have either come from America or Holland. They are even obtainable in pre-packed plastic bags and these, too, give very good results. It is well worth remembering that the mystique has been taken out of the lily and at least one of them—'Enchantment'—has become a garden plant to match the Nasturtium, both in colour and in ease of growth.

LILY—see Lilium

LIQUIDAMBER *styraciflua*—Sweet Gum
This is an excellent tree for the smaller garden. It can be grown as a specimen which will not become overpowering too soon, and it will provide interesting foliage throughout the summer—ivy shaped leaves—which give exciting autumn colour, varying from orange to

red to deep maroon, mahogany and black. When the leaves have fallen, the tree has a distinction of its own in its corklike bark and its upright shape—interesting to see against the winter skyline. Buy a plant, either open ground or in a container, in a size that suits your pocket, from a nursery or garden centre, and plant at any time in open weather from the end of October to the end of March.

LOBULARIA—Annual Alyssum

This is the high class name of the popular bedding plant which forms a neat mound of white flowers that go on throughout the summer. It is useful and beautiful if it is used with discretion—but when it becomes a long straight line of white dotted between African Marigolds, Zinnias and Lobelia, it is as boring as all the rest. It is grown and sold as a half-hardy annual but it will soon become naturalised and seedlings will grow which can be left to develop to maturity with careful weeding. One of its charms, which is often overlooked, is that it has a delightful honey scent. Either buy seeds, and sow them rather late—not before the end of April—or buy plants from a nursery, garden centre or shop and conserve their offspring. (There are many different varieties offered, but only the whites are worth growing. The alleged pinks are only a dirty puce and are 'more curious than beautiful'.)

LONICERA—Honeysuckle

The common Woodbine or Honeysuckle is one of our best native plants and it is well worth a place in the garden. But there are two varieties that are still more decorative, although there is little to choose between them—some people say they are virtually the same plant. You will find offered in nurseries and garden centres Lonicera 'Belgica' or the Early Dutch Honeysuckle and Lonicera 'Serotina' or the Late Dutch Honeysuckle. They both seem to flower at much the same time, producing honeysuckle blossoms that are cream touched with red, and well scented. These are followed by large red berries and, very often, flowers and berries are seen together. They are both deciduous, go on from June to September and can be used as climbing plants, on a fence or wall, or on tripods to give more flower in a confined space, or to ramble over some unsightly object. Lonicera *japonica*, the Japanese Honeysuckle, has given some interesting forms. One of these is called by the clumsy name of Lonicera *japonica aureo reticulata*. This is a variegated honeysuckle with evergreen leaves (in a mild winter) which has flowers rather like our own common honeysuckle, in pale yellow, and beautifully scented, while Lonicera *japonica* 'Halleana' is similar in flower but with bronzy leaves which are rather more evergreen, even when the wind blows cold. Do not have anything to do with the shrubby honeysuckle, Lonicera *nitida*, which was once planted widely as a hedge plant—unless you like clipping hedges. If it is to be a thing of beauty, it needs at least three clips a year. However, if you have one of those electrically driven machines, which you enjoy using, then it can make a very attractive neat hedge.

There are other shrubby honeysuckles which are well worth growing. These are Lonicera *fragrantissima*, Lonicera *standishii* and Lonicera 'Purpusii'. In order to save trouble in making a choice, Lonicera 'Purpusii', the hybrid between the first two, is the best. It gives its small, creamy, honeysuckle-scented flowers as early as February—sometimes January, in a mild winter. It is one of the essentials of the modern winter garden, which is made up of hardy plants that flower outside in the early part of the year. Even so, it is wise to plant it somewhere near the house in order that its perfume may be fully enjoyed, without having to walk through wet grass. The climbing varieties must be bought as pot grown or container grown plants, but the shrubby varieties, Lonicera *nitida*, *fragrantissima*, *standishii* and 'Purpusii' can be planted from open ground. All may be set at any time in open weather from the end of October to the end of March—but it is wiser to plant the winter flowering shrubby honeysuckles early in the year because there is a chance that you may be able to enjoy their beauty even when they are first planted.

LUNARIA—Honesty

You are more likely to find this biennial (see page 87) listed by seedsmen under its common name than under its Latin name. It is a singularly interesting plant—for nobody knows exactly where it originated, and whether or not it is a native plant. In my opinion, its greatest value is that it provides a mauvy-pink background to the Daffodils, but others prefer the beauty of its moon-like seedpods (hence the Latin name) which are transparent circles, of what appears to be Nature's plastic, containing a few seeds. It shows its Honesty by displaying the fact that it is bearing seeds. But much more than this, Honesty is an interesting plant to grow because it will seed itself all over the place. Once you have come to recognise the seedlings, it can be allowed to pop up anywhere with its flowers and seed heads, both of which are never out of place. Another strange habit is that although you may start off with a rosy-pink or mauvy-pink coloured form, suddenly one year all its seedlings will be pure white—then by some strange trick of genetics, the next year they will be pink again. Although Honesty is a biennial, plants are not offered for sale by nurseries, garden centres and shops, so it is necessary to grow your own from seed. Once started, provided you protect the self-sown plants that will arise, there is no need to sow again, only to transplant as necessary.

LUPIN—see Lupinus

LUPINUS—Lupin

The Russell Lupins were one of the few sensations of the horticultural world. When they were first shown in 1935, at the Royal Horticultural Society's June show, nothing like them had ever been seen before and they were an immediate success. They have tall full spikes in a wide range of colours and the flowers are held all round the spikes, staggering in their display in early June. Until recently, I would have recommended the purchase of mixed seedlings because these were, at one time, quite as good as the named varieties—but in my own experience it seems no longer to be true. I bought a batch when I replanted my herbaceous border recently and they were all dirty pinks and dull mauvy purples. It seems that it is better to choose named varieties—preferably those which you have seen in flower and like yourself. Many are still being raised and introduced and almost all are good, but they are more expensive than taking a chance on a mixed batch. If you cannot see them in flower, a short selection of the named sorts is: 'Blue Jacket', blue and white; 'Fireglow', orange and gold; 'George Russell'—named after the man who worked for nearly fifty years to produce them—double pink; 'Lady Gay', pale yellow; 'Mrs Noel Terry', pink; 'Nellie B. Allen', salmon orange; 'Thundercloud', purple and mauve; and 'Wheatsheaf', deep yellow touched with pink.

There is one other type of lupin that is worth mentioning, the Tree Lupin. This is really a shrub which can be grown in dry poor soil to give yellow flowers over a long period. And if you want to be really lazy, to produce a good show of flowers for little effort, combine the Tree Lupin with the everlasting pea. Russell Lupins may be bought from nurseries or garden centres as plants by name—or you can sow seed and hope for the best. Tree Lupins (Lupinus *arboreus*) should always be bought as plants from nurseries and they must either be pot or container grown. These are better set in the spring.

LYCHNIS—Maltese Cross—Rose Campion

Lychnis *chalcedonica* is the Maltese Cross, so called because of the shape of the individual flowers which are bright scarlet and make up a round head about 2 or 3in across. It is a fine old border plant to give some spots of bright colour from June to August. It grows to about 3ft with rough oval-shaped light-green leaves. Lychnis *coronaria* (formerly called Agrostemma *coronaria*) is the Rose Campion and one of the most attractive of all perennials. The stems and leaves are light silver-grey forming a plant about 2ft high which looks as if it had been constructed by an engineer. The dark-maroon flowers are produced in successive crops throughout the late summer. They are shown off to considerable advantage by the silver leaves and stems. Lychnis *viscaria* (or Viscaria *vulgaris*) is the German Catchfly and it is a dwarf growing plant which gets its name from the sticky substance on the stems which traps insects. Although it is called the German Catchfly it is a British plant and very easy to grow. It makes an excellent edging to a border with a mass of rose-red flowers and only grows about 1ft high. Perennials. Buy plants from a nursery or garden centre and set them in the spring.

MACLEAYA—Plume Poppy

Just why Macleaya *cordata* is called the Plume Poppy is hard to say— for it bears little resemblance to the oriental poppy. But it is a handsome plant growing to 6 or 7ft with long grey stems carrying silver leaves. The flowers are certainly plumes of pink—and the best variety is 'Kelways Coral Plume'. They have the considerable advantage of fading gracefully into attractive seed heads. However, there is one fault with this plan—it will not stand in water easily without the stems being boiled. Perennial. Buy plants from a nursery or garden centre and set them in the spring.

MAGNOLIA

If I follow the conditions of this book, strictly according to the qualifications of plants for performance in growth and performance in flower, there are only two magnolias that I should mention. These are Magnolia *sieboldii* (formerly called *parviflora*) and Magnolia *grandiflora*. Both are summer flowering, so they miss damage by spring frost which can destroy the earlier varieties. Magnolia *sieboldii* is a spreading shrub which will, in time, reach as much as 8 or 10ft and as much across—but that is in a very long time. It has interesting grey-green foliage and the flowers start in May but will continue, on and off, throughout the summer. They are very beautiful chalices of pure white with a red centre and a delightful scent. Magnolia *grandiflora*, as the name implies, has enormous flowers, rather like big water lilies, again produced during the summer in succession. It is a tall-growing evergreen plant with big leaves, larger than those of a laurel, and these are covered in a red down underneath. It can be grown on a wall, if it is trained, or as a specimen plant—even as a standard. It is relatively slow growing and is ideal as a specimen for the small garden.

Even though the spring flowering Magnolias may be damaged by frost, they are well worth the risk. Magnolia 'Soulangeana', the best known of them all, can be seen growing in what are now dingy London suburbs —like Wandsworth and Tooting. In fact, like a few other plants, they seem to enjoy a smoky, industrial climate. Magnolia 'Soulangeana' has tuliplike flowers in white with a faint touch of pink, Magnolia 'Soulangeana Nigra' is a deep reddish purple with, again, the habit of producing a few flowers later in the summer, and Magnolia 'Lennei' is a large flowered variety, again in the tulip shape, and in deep purple. The difficulty, in the past, with Magnolias has been transplanting. They do not move readily from the open ground—but if open ground plants are bought from a nursery they must have a root ball holding soil and tied up in sacking. They are better planted in the late spring than at any other time. Nowadays, container grown plants can be obtained from garden centres and these are more easily transplanted—always provided they have been grown in the container, rather than having been hastily put into them ready for spring sales. The way to test this is to examine the soil—if it is well settled, perhaps with a thin film of moss or weed growing over the top, then the plants are truly established in those containers and will move easily. If not, they should be avoided. Another way to find out if they are likely to be successful is to pick them up by the branches and if they hold the container, and the soil in it, without any suggestion of breakage, they are in the right condition for transplanting. But if they should be in any way loose, and show an inclination to leave the container and the soil behind, they should be avoided. Buy plants from a nursery or garden centre and set them in the spring, if from the open ground—but container grown plants may also be planted in the autumn.

MAHONIA

Only one of the Mahonias has a common name—Mahonia *aquifolium* (see page 70) is called the Oregon Grape because of the attractive berries it produces in the autumn. This is one of the easiest shrubs to grow and well measures up to the standard of this book. It has bronzy evergreen foliage which is even more attractive in the winter than it is in the summer. In the early spring it starts to produce its bunches of yellow flowers, and these are followed by the black grapes covered in a bloom which gives the plant its name. It has many uses. It can be grown as a low hedge, it can be used as ground cover, it can be planted as a specimen on its own—and its foliage is of great use for floral arrangement. Mahonia 'Undulata', the name indicates the shape of the leaves which are undulating, is a plant of doubtful origin, which makes it sound rather less attractive than it is. It is probably a hybrid of Mahonia *aquifolium* with some other species and it grows much taller—reaching a height of 6 or 8ft. It has the same bunch of yellow flowers in the early spring, followed by berries which are not, it must be admitted, as freely borne as those of Mahonia *aquifolium*. Even so, it is an effective shrub and, again, useful for flower arrangements. But the best of all is Mahonia *japonica*, a plant which has been grown in Japan for many years for decoration. This, like the others, has long sprays of hollylike leaves but the flowers are different. They are bunches of yellow lily-of-the-valley and they have the same equally attractive scent. The berries

98

are not quite as decorative, but the fact that the flowers are produced from as early as December through to April makes it one of the most valuable plants for the winter garden. An interesting point about Mahonia *japonica* is that if it is planted in the shade the leaves will be a rich, lustrous green—but if it is planted in full sunlight, they become yellow and orange. This state is not admired by the true plantsman, the real gardener, but it is, undoubtedly, very useful to the flower arranger. Buy plants from a nursery or garden centre, which may either be open ground or container grown, and set them in the spring.

MALUS—Crab

The Malus, the Ornamental Crabs are for everyone, everywhere—always provided you can keep the birds from eating the buds. The damage caused by birds is worse than any other single pest but, unfortunately for the gardeners, there is so much sympathy for the birds that they are allowed to ravage our plantations and orchards as much as they please. Consequently, the ornamental crabs, like other flowering trees, are at their best in towns, or near main roads, somewhere where the birds cannot attack them. But if they are planted in country gardens where there are hedges and woodlands in the near vicinity, then all the buds can be stripped. There will be no flower and, sometimes, very little growth. However, provided this difficulty can be overcome there are many of the malus which are generally attractive as small trees or large shrubs. Malus *floribunda* will make a very attractive small tree with a semi-weeping habit, producing a great show of small white flowers, faintly touched with pink, followed by yellow crab apples. Malus 'Atrosanguinea' is similar, but with flowers in a deeper colour. Malus 'Profusion' is a red flowered form with a few dark red berries and an attractive scent. If you want fruit, in preference to flower, then choose Malus 'John Downie' which has a small apple blossom type flower followed by crabs that are yellow, orange and red, and very useful for making crab apple jelly. But one of the best, although not one of the most plentiful is Malus *columnaria* 'Charlottae'. This has semi-double shell-pink flowers, deliciously scented, and not open until late May or early June. It is not a strong growing tree and so is very suitable for the smaller garden. Buy plants from a nursery or garden centre, either from the open ground or container grown, and set them at any time from the end of October until the end of March.

MARCH

Some species and varieties of the following plants flower in March: Bergenia, Camellia, Chaenomeles, Crocus, Doronicum, Erica, Forsythia, Galanthus, Garrya, Hamamelis, Iris, Jasminum, Narcissus, Primula, Prunus, Sarcococca, Vinca.

MARIGOLD—see Calendula and Tagetes

MARJORAM—see Origanum

MAUVE

Some species and varieties of the following plants have mauve flowers: Aster, Aubrieta, Buddleia, Campanula, Centaurea, Clarkia, Colchicum, Crocus, Cytisus, Dianthus, Echinops, Galega, Geranium, Hebe, Iris, Lamium, Lathyrus, Lavendula, Lunaria, Lupinus, Nepeta, Perowskia, Petunia, Primula, Salvia.

MAY

Some species and varieties of the following plants flower in May: Alyssum, Aubrieta, Berberis, Bergenia, Camellia, Centaurea, Chaenomeles, Clematis, Cytisus, Euphorbia, Genista, Kerria, Laburnum, Lunaria, Lupin (end of May), Malus, Myosotis, Narcissus, Paeonia, Primula, Prunus, Rheum, Ribes, Rosmarinus, Salvia, Syringa, Tamarix, Viburnum, Vinca, Weigela.

MEDIUM

Some species and varieties of the following annuals, perennials and shrubs grow to medium height—that is, between 2ft and 3½ft. All useful for the centre of a mixed or specialised border.

Annuals: Calendula, Centaurea, Clarkia, Delphinium (Larkspur), Lavatera, Tagetes.

Perennials: Achillea, Alstroemeria, Anemone, Angelica (will reach 4ft), Aster, Campanula, Chrysanthemum, Coreopsis, Euphorbia,

Geranium, Gypsophila, Helenium, Helianthus, Hemerocallis, Inula, Iris, Melissa, Monarda, Oenothera, Paeonia, Papaver, Perowskia, Phlox, Phygelius, Physostegia, Polygonatum, Salvia, Solidago.

Shrubs: Chaenomeles, Cistus, Cytisus (if pruned as instructed), Deutzia, Fuchsia, Hebe, Lavandula, Mahonia, Potentilla, Prunus, Ruta, Salvia, Senecio, Skimmia, Spiraea.

Bulbs: Gladiolus, Lilium.

MELISSA *officinalis*—Balm

One of the pleasures in the garden is to brush your hand through aromatic leaves to enjoy their scent. Balm is one of the best plants for this purpose, for its leaves are deliciously lemon scented and can be used for flavouring salads and salad dressings. It grows to about 3ft and flowers in July with bunches of small white flowers. These are not particularly attractive, but the bees love them. It must be very easy to grow because the Royal Horticultural Society's *Dictionary of Gardening* warns that it might be difficult in damp acid soil—which is just where I have it growing myself and it has become almost a weed. There is an attractive golden form, which is not as prolific but equally well scented. Buy plants, usually from the herb shelf, in a garden shop or garden centre and set them in the spring.

MENTHA—Mint

Many herbs can be decorative as well as useful, and the Variegated Mint is one of the best of all—its official title is Mentha *rotundifolia variegata*. It grows to a height of about 18in or 2ft, if left on its own. It is a fine variegated foliage plant for the mixed border or the herbaceous border. It is best for use with new potatoes. Buy plants from a nursery or garden centre or specialist herb farm and set them in the spring.

MINT—see Mentha

MISCANTHUS

Contrast is always desirable, and where there are many flat-leaved plants something that stands upright creates an interesting variation.

This can be found in grasses and bamboos—although bamboos are rather dangerous because they may soon take over a whole garden. The Miscanthus are strong-growing perennial grasses and may need dividing every three years, but they are not as rampant as the bamboos. Miscanthus *sinensis* variety 'Gracillimus' is a grass that grows to about 4ft with very narrow leaves which are slim and graceful. Miscanthus *sinensis* 'Variegatus' is somewhat similar, with rather wider leaves, and they are striped with white for the whole of their length. I would advise you to avoid the variety called Miscanthus *sinensis* 'Zebrinus' which has similar leaves but banded crosswise with yellow. This, to my mind, gives a somewhat unnatural effect. These are all perennial plants, dying down every year. Buy them from a nursery or garden centre and set them at any time from the end of October to the middle of April.

MONARDA—Bee Balm or Bergamot
This is a perennial with flowers that resemble sea anemones. It has two uses. It gives colour, and a different form of flower in June and July in the herbaceous or mixed border and the leaves can also be used for flavouring tea. I understand that it is one of the essential ingredients in the famous Earl Grey mixture. There are a number of good varieties, the best are, undoubtedly, 'Cambridge Scarlet' and 'Croftway Pink'. Buy plants from a nursery or garden centre and set them at any time in open weather from November to April.

MONTBRETIA—see Crocosmia

MUSCARI—Grape Hyacinth—Musk Hyacinth—Starch Hyacinth
It would be wrong to give a false idea about the Grape Hyacinth. One of the other common names, the Musk Hyacinth—with its suggestion of an exciting perfume—only refers to a particular species which, unfortunately, is rather tender and cannot be grown easily out of doors all the year round. But the other varieties, with their small blue flowers, held in spikes, like upright bunches of tiny grapes, are easy to grow in almost any position. Most of them are blue and there are several different species and varieties but the true blues are best. Muscari 'Heavenly Blue' flowers in April with sky blue blossoms.

Muscari 'Tubergenianum' which is known as the Oxford and Cambridge Muscari has two colours—the top is light blue, and the base of the flower is dark blue. Both grow to about 9in high and they should be planted 3in deep. Buy bulbs and plant them in the autumn.

MYOSOTIS—Forget-me-not

This is another plant which is strictly according to the conditions of this book. It is so easy to grow that it will seed itself all around, even in the paths. It is a delight with daffodils and will go on flowering for a long time afterwards. It is a biennial, but it does not need the careful treatment that has to be given to other plants of the same type. When you start to grow Forget-me-nots, you should buy seed and sow in May or June for flowering the following year. Having once obtained the plants, there is little need to do very much more, for they will

Myosotis (Forget-me-not)

reproduce themselves in many places. However, to be certain of a fresh stock the method of propagation is simple. When the Forget-me-nots are over, pull them out and lay them down in a shady place. The seeds will drop and germinate and you will then have hundreds, thousands even, of young plants.

NARCISSUS—Narcissus—Daffodil—Jonquil—Pheasant Eye
There are so many Narcissi, from the tiny Hoop Petticoat daffodils to the big bouncing flowers of the florists, that it is hard to know where to begin. They can be grown in so many ways—forced in pots to flower at Christmas time or they can be naturalised in fields. They can be bedded out in borders, to go on flowering year after year, or they can be used for the sequence of flowers in bedding out that is now almost solely practised by public parks.

At the present time, nobody is quite sure which are the best varieties for naturalising. There are trials going on in the Royal Horticultural Society's gardens at Wisley to discover which are the best to leave to their own devices in long grass and to find which can be planted in lawns and mown down, without harm. The results will not be known until about 1978 or 1980, when it will be wise to consult the journals of the Royal Horticultural Society to find the best varieties for this rough treatment.

Yet there are a few known to be satisfactory under almost any conditions. And it is best if I start with the dwarf daffodils which are so easy to grow, offer so much charm, and yet—curiously enough—are so often neglected.

The best of all for naturalising is one that grows wild in this country. This is called the Tenby Daffodil or, more correctly, Narcissus obvallaris. It is a miniature trumpet daffodil, reaching about 10in, and it can be grown wild in grass where it will continue to increase and give pleasure, year after year, with no attention.

Narcissus cyclamineus is another dwarf wild form, but not a native of this country. It has petals which are flung back, like those of the wild cyclamen—which is why it is so named. There are many different varieties of the true species and several hybrids. They are all good but the type itself is cheap—which means that it is plentiful—this, in turn, means that it grows freely and is the best to buy.

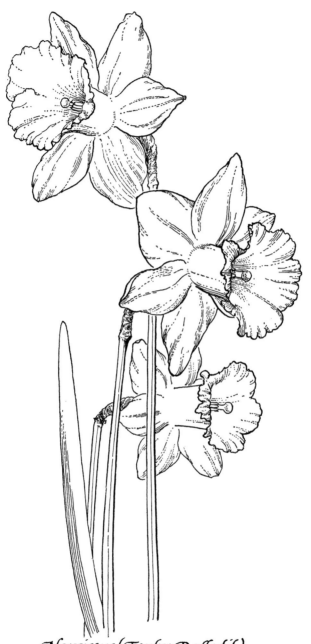

Narcissus (Tenby Daffodil)

Narcissus *pseudo-narcissus* is the long Latin name of another of our own wild plants—the Lent Lily. It is not a plant that grows everywhere for it likes a position which is fairly damp. Like the Tenby daffodil it is a miniature replica of the large flowered, trumpet daffodils.

Narcissus *jonquilla*, the Jonquil, is one of our oldest garden plants. It is a yellow daffodil growing to about 12in but its greatest charm is its scent, for this is the very essence of spring. It lasts well in flower in the open, cuts well, reproduces itself freely, and is cheap to buy.

When it comes to the larger flowered and taller growing daffodils there are many more variations than just a straight yellow trumpet. It is even possible to buy a red daffodil, if you should happen to want one, and the current price is around £350 per bulb. But not many people have this bizarre taste—or this amount of money—and until the results of the Royal Horticultural Society's trials of daffodils suitable for naturalising are completed, the following is a list of good varieties which cost very much less than the red daffodil and are all good garden plants.

The most famous yellow trumpet daffodil is 'King Alfred', self coloured in deep yellow. However, it is a little doubtful if the true 'King Alfred' exists nowadays, but bulbs bought under this name from a reliable specialist supplier will still give a good performance. A newer introduction is 'Golden Harvest', similar and slightly larger. These two are really showy but bigger flowers are liable to more damage from rain and wind than those that are not quite so magnificent. 'Kingscourt' is a trumpet daffodil, rather smaller than the first two, but of good colour with a trumpet that is slightly deeper than the petals. White daffodils can be very attractive, especially when they are planted among roses which have bright red young foliage, for the leaves of the roses stand up like flowers above the white daffodils. The best of all the white trumpet daffodils is 'Mount Hood'. There are several different forms of the flowers that are popularly known as Narcissi, although this is the correct generic name for all daffodils. 'Carlton' is typical with broad soft yellow petals backing a large clear yellow crown. It flowers freely and is one of the few that is already known to naturalise well. Narcissi are distinguished by a number of varieties which have deep cups on pale petals. 'Fortune' is one of the best with a rich orange cup on soft yellow petals—again, very hardy and good for growing in the garden. Looking as if it is almost half way between a trumpet daffodil and a narcissus, because of its large cup of pale orange, 'Duke of Windsor' has a nice contrast in colour, for the cup is backed by white petals. A late flowering variety which not only grows well in the garden but still wins prizes at flower shows, is 'Kilworth'—white petals holding a cup of bright orange. 'Tudor Minstrel' carries a large flower —nearly 5in across—with white pointed petals backing a well formed cup of rich yellow. There is a certain old-world charm about double daffodils—'Irene Copeland' has a full double flower with long white petals, interspersed with others of apricot, fading to pale yellow. The flower lasts well, both when it is cut and when it is in the garden, and the bulbs reproduce themselves freely. One of the oldest of all the true narcissi is the ancient Pheasant's Eye which has been grown in our gardens for nearly 400 years. It has a small cup of yellow, rimmed with red, on white petals—and it is delightfully scented. Buy bulbs from a good bulb merchant and plant them from middle of September to the end of October, 4 to 6in deep according to the size of the bulb.

NEPETA—Catmint

The Catmint is a delightful perennial for edging borders. Its silvery leaves and soft mauve flowers make an excellent foil for the other plants. The variety that is best known is called, generally, Nepeta 'Mussinii'—but this is not its correct name. It should be called Nepeta 'Faasenii' and an improved variety is 'Six Hills Giant'. Buy plants from a nursery or garden centre and set them in the spring, preferably in April.

NOVEMBER

Some species and varieties of the following plants flower in November, or they have berries, seedheads or good autumn foliage: Amelanchier, Aucuba, Berberis, Bergenia, Calendula, Chrysanthemum, Cortaderia, Cotoneaster, Crocus, Erica, Euonymus, Hedera, Hydrangea, Ilex, Jasminum, Leycesteria, Liquidamber, Lunaria, Mahonia, **Malus,** Physalis, Prunus, Pyracantha, Quercus, Rhus, Rubus, **Rudbeckia,** Skimmia, Sorbus, Viburnum, Vitis.

OAK—see Quercus

OCTOBER

Some species and varieties of the following plants flower in October, or they have berries, seedheads or good autumn foliage: Alchemilla, Amelanchier, Anemone, Aster, Aucuba, Berberis, Bergenia, Calendula, Ceratostigma, Chrysanthemum, Colchicum, Cortaderia, Cotoneaster, Crocosmia, Dianthus, Elaeagnus, Epilobium, Fatshedera, Fatsia, Fuchsia, Hebe, Hedera, Hydrangea, Ilex, Leycesteria, Liquidamber, Lunaria, Macleaya, Malus, Petunia, Physalis, Polygonum, Prunus, Pyracantha, Quercus, Rhus, Rudbeckia, Skimmia, Sorbus, Spartium, Spiraea, Tropaeolum, Vitis.

OENOTHERA—Evening Primrose

This is not the wild plant that can be seen growing on banks and in meadows, but the perennial form from the United States of America. It is an excellent garden plant for it gives a really good show for two months without a break. Planted near one of the blue geraniums—either Geranium *pratense coeruleum plenum* or Geranium 'A. T. Johnson' —there is no more delightful combination for the months of June and July. The species that has given the best hybrids is called Oenothera *fruticosa* and it comes from Nova Scotia. Oenothera *fruticosa major* has large flowers, as the name implies, O. *f.* 'William Cuthbertson' and O. *f.* 'Fraserii' are also large and grow to about 18in. Oenothera 'Fireworks' is a shorter grower, at about 15in, and has bright yellow flowers, with a stripe of red on the back, and the stems are also red— which makes it decorative even when it is out of flower. There is a very dwarf form called Oenothera *missouriensis* which is known in America as the Osark Sundrop. It has large pale-yellow flowers about 2–2½in across and it only grows to about 9in. Perennial. Buy plants from a nursery or garden centre and set them in the spring.

OLEARIA *haastii*

This shrub which comes from New Zealand is not, perhaps, spectacular but it does have a use in the garden. It grows naturally to a neat rounded shape and is an excellent evergreen for a formal position reaching about 5ft high and as much across. It flowers in August when it covers itself in small white daisies. However, these should be trimmed off with the shears, as soon as they have faded, because the seed heads are

Oenothera

untidy. Buy plants from a nursery or garden centre, either open ground or container grown, and set them at any time in open weather from October to March.

ORANGE

Some species and varieties of the following plants have orange flowers: Alstroemeria, Begonia, Berberis, Buddleia, Calendula, Chrysanthemum, Crocosmia, Cytisus, Euphorbia, Gaillardia, Helenium, Helianthemum, Hemerocallis, Lilium, Lupin, Papaver, Phlox, Phygelius, Physalis, Potentilla, Rose, Tropaeolum.

ORIGANUM

Origanum *vulgare* is the plant we know better as Marjoram. It is as useful in the garden as it is in the kitchen—where the leaves give a delightful flavour to stews. It is also decorative, with small flowers rather like those of a heliotrope, but if they are allowed to develop, there is less growth, and so fewer leaves for flavouring. Buy plants from a nursery or garden centre and set them in the spring or sow seed at the end of March or beginning of April. One of the best of all dual-purpose plants is the golden form—Origanum *vulgare aureum*. For this has golden foliage which stays a good colour for a long time, and the leaves can be used for flavouring just as well as those of the ordinary herb. This cannot be grown from seed and must be bought as a plant.

OSMANTHUS

Osmanthus *delavayii* is an attractive evergreen flowering shrub that grows to between 6 and 8ft with small leaves rather like those of a box tree, only they are slightly cut at the edges. It flowers in April when the branches are covered with small white flowers which look as if they had been made of porcelain. The scent is charming—very fresh and clean. All of the plants now in cultivation are developed from one that grew in the nursery of Mons Maurice de Vilmorin in Paris in 1890, from seed sent back from China by the Abbé Delavay. A much more common plant is now known as Osmanthus *heterophyllum*, but it may be more easily found in catalogues and garden centres as Osmanthus *aquifolium* or even *ilicifolium*—two of its names which are still widely used. There are several varieties of this strong-growing evergreen with leaves like a holly, but there is only one worth considering as the others are somewhat dull. Osmanthus *heterophyllus purpurea* is one of the very few evergreens with purple foliage. This is useful in the garden as a contrast and also for flower arrangement. Buy plants from a nursery or garden centre and set them at any time between the end of October and the middle of April.

PAEONIA—Peony

If there is one thing that might possibly exclude the Peony from this book it is the length of time it takes to flower. Some people say that it is as long as three to five years before Peonies will really flower satisfactorily—but I have found that if good sized plants are bought they usually give a fair show in the second year. However, this possible disadvantage turns out to be an advantage in the end—for once Peonies are planted they will go on quite happily for thirty years without any more attention. The flowers are very decorative and beautifully scented. The foliage makes good ground cover and is also interesting in its own right when the flowers have faded.

The oldest Peony of all is Paeonia *officinalis rubra plena*—the old double red of the cottage gardens. This plant is hard to kill and many of the fine clumps that give such a wonderful show of flower in May have been handed down from generation to generation. Incidentally there are a number of varieties which can be obtained: 'China Rose', 'Salmon Rose', 'Crimson Globe', an intense red with single flowers, and P. *officinalis mutabilis*, similar to the old double red, but with rich pink flowers that change to white as they mature.

The large flowered Chinese varieties are only new in comparison with the old double red and, for that matter, very few that are grown today were raised in China. The period of their introduction can be judged by the name of one of the best—'Sarah Bernhardt'. This is a very large blush pink of some grandeur, and it would seem to be very suitably named. 'Bowl of Beauty' is another attractive variety with carmine petals and yellow centre, 'Lady Derby' is a double pink and 'Snow Clouds' is ivory white with a faint touch of pink when it first opens. These flower in June and July. They are all perennials and you should buy plants from a nursery or garden centre and set them in the autumn.

PAPAVER—Poppy

The big perennial oriental poppies stand up well to the conditions inherent in this book for they positively resent feeding and enjoy neglect and poor soil. There is just one thing—they are floppy and they give a better display, and take up less room, with the support of a few pea sticks. There are several very good varieties—'King George' is a scarlet, 'Mrs Perry' is a shrimp pink, 'Perry's White' is described by the name and 'Salmon Glow' is a good salmon.

The Shirley poppies are hardy annuals which are usually supplied as mixed seedlings and make a magnificent show in colours that range from white to scarlet throughout the late summer. They were all developed by the Rev W. Wilks of Shirley, near Croydon in Surrey, from one plant of the common corn poppy which he found in the corner of a field. Buy seeds which should be sown in February, where the plants are to stand, and thin out to 9in apart.

Iceland poppies are varieties and developments of Papaver *nudicaule* which does come from sub-arctic regions. They can be treated either as hardy annuals, biennials or they will occasionally behave like perennials. But the best method of growing them is to sow seed in August and plant out in October. You will then have flowers the next year from May to September. The best strain is the 'Meadhome Strain', obtainable from Home Meadows Nursery, Martlesham, Suffolk. The colours are positively brilliant—yellow, orange, pink and red.

PEACH—see Prunus

PEROWSKIA *atriplicifolia*

This shrub, with the curious name derived from the Russian who discovered it, behaves like a perennial because it dies down to the ground each year. It grows about 2–3ft, and from the end of July to September it forms a blue haze of flowers which are enhanced by the white dust that covers the stems. It prefers a position that is hot and dry, but it will grow in the poorest of soils without trouble. Strictly speaking a shrub, it is sold by nurserymen who specialise in perennials. Buy plants, preferably pot grown, from a nursery or garden centre and set in the spring.

Petunias

PETUNIA

The Petunia is the half-hardy annual, sold as a bedding-out plant, yet it almost comes up to the standard of the nasturtium. It is useful in so many ways. It is a great gap filler—if a spot in the border is found to be bare (mistakes occur even in the best regulated gardens) a petunia can be bought in a pot and planted—even when it is in flower. It will then give a good display right through the summer until the frosts. It is an excellent plant for urns and vases, and if two or three separate colours are chosen a startling bedding-out scheme can be devised in an abstract pattern which will be colourful from June to September. Nowadays there are a great many Petunias in all sorts of shapes and colours. It is best to avoid some of the more flamboyant varieties with frilly edges and big double flowers. These do not stand up to an average English summer. They become little more than the floral equivalent of a woman in a dressing gown after a shower of rain. But there are a few which are known as the Resisto strain which have been specially bred to stand up to wet weather and wind. But it may not be possible to buy these as grown plants which, unfortunately, puts them out of the scope of this book because it is not written for those who wish to indulge in the intricacies—and the work—of sowing seeds in heat, pricking out and hardening off. However, they are so good that it is worth trying to grow your own Resisto petunias by germinating them on a radiator and hardening them off on a window sill. But if you are prepared to take a chance on the summer, then buy plants of any strain—singles for preference—from a nursery or garden centre and set them when all risk of frost is past. You will find that plants grown in individual pots are considerably more expensive than those grown in boxes and supplied wrapped up in a bit of newspaper—but they are well worth the extra money.

PHILADELPHUS—Mock Orange

These are old fashioned shrubs which have been with us for many years. The common name was given to them because it was said the scent of the flowers resembles that of orange blossom—which it does, very nearly, but not quite. They are mostly white, and some have dark blotches at the base of the petal. But there are only two that really matter so far as garden decoration is concerned. Philadelphus 'Virginale' is a strong growing shrub which will reach 10 or 12ft high by 10 or 12ft wide carrying a mass of double flowers with the well known delicious scent in early June. Philadelphus *coronarius aurea* is a single-flowered plant, again with scented white flowers, but with the additional attraction of gold foliage that lasts well through the summer. Both of these give a better performance if they are pruned as soon as they have finished flowering by cutting out the old wood. Buy plants, either open ground or container grown, from a nursery or garden centre and set them at any time from the beginning of November to the end of March.

PHLOX

These well known perennials have no common name. There are two kinds—the tall perennial varieties, forms of Phlox *paniculata*, and dwarf spreading plants which are all variations of Phlox *decussata*. The tall perennials have been bred extensively in recent years but, fortunately, the scent remains with them all—an intriguing, slightly peppery perfume as delicious indoors as it is in the garden. They are obtainable in almost any colour but those that are too bright fade easily in the sun. However, the best of these is an old variety called 'Brigadier', a bright orange which seems to be fairly tough. Other good varieties are 'Dresden China', a soft pink with a deeper shading round the eye—one of the attractions of many of the phlox flowers; 'Fairy's Petticoat' is an intriguing shade of soft mulberry purple; 'Lilac Time' is a lilac; 'Othello' a dark red; 'Salmon Glow' is described by the name but it has the addition of a white eye; and 'Snowstorm' is almost whiter than white. They are all perennials, buy plants from a nursery or garden centre and set them in the spring.

PHYGELIUS *capensis*—Cape Figwort

Officially, the Cape Figwort is a shrub but it dies back every year to the ground, even in a mild winter, which makes it behave like a perennial. The roots remain unharmed. In the following year it throws up growths to 2 or 3ft carrying bright orange snapdragon flowers during the summer. There is only one consideration—it must have sun if it is to give of its best. Buy plants, preferably in pots, from a nursery or garden centre and set them in the spring.

PHYLLYREA *decora*

This graceful evergreen is not used now as much as it should be. It is rather like an elegant laurel, growing in layers, with outward spreading branches and long narrow dark-green leaves. In the autumn, it carries white flowers which, although they are insignificant, have a certain charm. It can be used in the garden as a spreading evergreen to give emphasis in the winter and it is also particularly valuable for floral arrangement. It makes a fairly large bush, as much as 5 or 6ft high and 7 or 8ft through if it is left to grow unchecked. However, a little judicious pruning with secateurs can keep it to much the size that you require. Buy plants from a nursery or garden centre and set them in the early autumn or in the spring.

PHYSALIS *franchetti*—Cape Gooseberry or Chinese Lantern

This plant lives well up to the standard of this book—because it is very decorative and so strong growing that it can be a nuisance when it settles down in a place it likes. Its chief attraction is the balloonlike calyx which surrounds the fruit that forms after the flower is over. This will last some time into the winter, when it becomes naturally skeletonised and is still interesting to look at. Cut just at the right time, when they have ripened and before the colour begins to fade, these big orange-red bubbles can be hung up to dry for winter decoration. Buy plants from a nursery or garden centre and set them in the spring.

PHYSOSTEGIA—Obedient Plant

This good perennial is worth growing for its gimmick alone—it is a flower that amuses the children. The reason for the common name, the Obedient Plant, is that the flowers can be moved to any position and they will stay there. Quite apart from this, it is a decorative plant for the herbaceous or mixed border growing to about 2ft and flowering in August and September. The best known is the variety 'Vivid', but this is something of an exaggeration, for it is a pale pink. Buy plants from a nursery or garden centre and set them in the spring.

PICEA—Spruce

The Spruce is largely included because if you order a Picea *abies* from a nursery or buy one from a garden centre, you will be buying a nursery grown Christmas tree with good roots. It will then be possible to use this year after year because its root system will be fibrous and compact, better able to stand transplanting than a rough tree dug up without care for the Christmas trade. There are also countless dwarf forms, like Picea *abies* 'Clanbrasiliana' and Picea *abies* 'Dumosa' which are good dwarf plants for the rock garden. Buy plants from a nursery or garden centre and set them at any time in open weather from October to April.

PINK (the flower)—see Dianthus

PINK (the colour)

Some species and varieties of the following plants have pink flowers: Anemone, Aster, Aubrieta, Begonia, Bergenia, Campanula, Centaurea, Chaenomeles, Chrysanthemum, Clarkia, Clematis, Crocosmia, Cytisus, Delphinium, Deutzia, Dianthus, Digitalis, Epilobium, Erica, Escallonia, Fuchsia, Geranium, Gladiolus, Godetia, Gypsophila, Heliantheum, Hemerocallis, Hibiscus, Lathyrus, Lavatera, Lilium, Lupinus, Macleaya, Malus, Paeonia, Papaver, Petunia, Phlox, Primula, Prunus, Ribes, Rose, Saxifraga, Sedum, Spiraea, Tulipa, Verbascum, Viburnum, Weigela.

PLUM—see Prunus

POLYANTHUS—see Primula

POLYGONATUM *multiflorum*—Solomon's Seal—Lady's Seal—
David's Harp

This native plant is a happy combination of habit, foliage and flower. It carries arching sprays of grey-green leaves which, alone, are attractive and they bear hanging white bells in June. It grows to about 2ft high and is easy in any soil—and almost indestructible. Buy plants from a nursery or garden centre and set them in the spring.

POLYGONUM

There are two sorts of Polygonum—a climber and some herbaceous perennials. The climber goes by the long and complicated name of Polygonum *baldschuanicum* and is known commonly as the Russian Vine. It is the fastest growing climber of any. It will put on as much as 15ft of growth in a year and it has been said, by nursery workers, that it is dangerous to stand near it because it may well entwine you with its fast-moving tendrils. It is an invaluable plant for covering an eyesore but, unfortunately, it will not grow over corrugated iron. It can be set to grow and ramble through an old tree to give a fine show of its white flowers just faintly touched with pink throughout the summer—but it must have room to grow. Buy plants, which must be pot or container grown, from a nursery or garden centre and set them at any time in open weather from October to April.

There are several herbaceous perennial Polygonums but one stands out above all others—Polygonum *amplexicaule atrosanguineum*. This, too, is a long flowering plant, producing spikes of red flowers from June right through to October. It grows to about 4ft and has very strong tough roots. It will grow almost anywhere, and in the places that it likes it will romp away and may need keeping in check. Polygonum *cuspidatum* is a tall, strong plant which must be watched in case it runs a little too far. Even so, the long stems carry big heart-shaped leaves, which are very impressive, and hanging bunches of flowers, 4–5in long, from July to October. Even after that, the bare stems are attractive in the winter. Buy plants of these perennial species from a nursery or garden centre and set them at any time in open weather from October to April.

POPPY—see Papaver

POTENTILLA—Cinquefoil

As with the Polygonums, there are two forms—shrubs and perennials. There are many different varieties of the shrubby form of Potentilla, called Potentilla *fruticosa* and they make compact rounded bushes up to 4 or 5ft high. Their chief characteristic is that they give a continuous show of flower throughout the summer. That is to say, they do not produce one glorious burst of blossom, as is the habit of many flowering shrubs, but they give crop after crop of flowers which may not be so immediately spectacular but make a strong contribution to the colour of the garden for a long time. Furthermore, they keep their leaves very late into the winter which makes them useful in the general pattern of the garden when the flowers are over. My own favourite is Potentilla 'Vilmoriniana', a white, but it has the most attractive silvery-grey leaves and is worth growing for these alone. 'Moonlight' ('Maanelys') flowering from May to September is a yellow and 'Purdomi' is a dwarf with big yellow flowers. Several new varieties have been introduced recently with stronger coloured flowers. 'Tangerine' was the first and when it is planted in the shade it will produce flowers that really are the colour of the name. 'Sunset' is a variation and one or two more have been introduced recently.

The perennials are neat plants growing to a height of about 2ft and flowering from June to September. 'Gibson's Scarlet' is a single blood red, 'Mons Rouillard' is a double—red and yellow, and 'Yellow Queen' is a bright yellow. Buy both the shrubs and the perennials from a nursery or garden centre and set them at any time in open weather from October to April.

PRIMULA

There are countless varieties of all sorts of Primulas which vary between tender greenhouse plants and hardy alpines for rock gardens. But only two qualify for this book—the Primrose and the Polyanthus (see page 87). And the Primrose, although it is a native plant only just scrapes in—because it is one of those plants that grows well in some places and not in others. For example, I have a stream running through my garden and Primroses grow on the bank facing north and Violets on the bank facing south—but never the other way about. There are plenty of cultivated forms of the Primrose to be obtained from different nurseries and seedsmen but many of these are outlandish—in strange colours, with double flowers and other peculiar variations. None of them are as beautiful as the ordinary wild Primrose. But it is possible to obtain cultivated plants through one or two nurseries. However, this is not very easy so I give the name and address of the nursery that can supply these plants—Mrs Hazel Key, Geranium Nurseries, Evesham, Worcestershire. The polyanthus demonstrates the power of hybrid vigour. It is a cross between the Cowslip, the Oxslip and the Primrose. Nowadays, there are many beautiful strains with very large flowers in various colours—including mauve and blue. However, the bigger and brighter they are, the more difficult they are to grow. The best method of growing Polyanthus is to buy a mixed batch, plant them in your border and leave them in position. Do not take all the trouble of planting and replanting that is generally recommended. The result of leaving them where they are will mean that some will die and others will survive. After three years take those that have survived and divide them and these will be the plants that will suit the conditions of your garden and go on flowering year after year, in the same place. In my own garden, I have developed a strain with very deep magenta-red flowers which seems to be ideal for my soil and they are good perennials lasting for years. The time to plant is in the early autumn and plants may be obtained from nurseries, garden centres and garden shops.

PRIVET—see Ligustrum

PRUNUS

This is a vast family which includes the Almond, the Cherry, the Laurel, the Peach and the Plum. Apart from the Laurel, which is a good evergreen, all the rest are excellent flowering trees for garden decoration. Nowadays, there is only one snag—the birds. The depredations of bullfinches and bluetits in country districts have caused many of the ornamental members of the prunus family to become barren. The birds hide up in the trees and hedgerows and then fly out to strip the flower buds systematically, branch by branch. There are several ways of overcoming this—and really keen gardeners, who care little for birds, recommend a shotgun. But as so many houses are built in small groups, or in estates, there is less risk to the buds because the birds are frightened away by the people and the traffic. If you happen to live on a fairly busy road you will always be able to enjoy these blossoms which are the very essence of spring. It is a little difficult to classify so many plants and perhaps the best way to describe them is in alphabetical order under their common names—but leaving the Laurels to last.

Almond: The Common Almond is now correctly known as Prunus *dulcis*. It is also called Prunus *amygdalus* and Prunus *communis*, although these names have been superseded. The almond has been grown here since the sixteenth century and there are few trees more pretty, either in town or country, in the early spring—usually about the middle of April. Even in the heart of London, the Almond will freely produce its pink buds followed by white flowers—and often in advance of trees growing in the country. D. H. Lawrence has written a very beautiful poem about almond trees, describing the gnarled and twisted branches which are transformed by the flowers. The dwarf Russian Almond, Prunus *tenella* is a neat shrub growing to about 2ft and the best variety is 'Fire Hill', with bright rose red flowers, a form that grows in the Balkan Alps.

The Flowering Cherries: Prunus *avium fl. pl.* is the double form of the wild Gean. It is one of the most decorative of all the flowering cherries and a strong grower. Furthermore, it has the advantage that the buds are distasteful to the birds. Prunus *incisa*, the Mount Fuji Cherry, is a neat bush which can be grown as a standard tree. It carries an abundance of small white flowers which appear to be shaded with pink because of the red calyx that holds the petals in position. It came here, originally, as a dwarfed Bonsai specimen which grew away from its restricted root run to prove that it was a good garden plant. There are two varieties worth noting, one is called 'Praecox' and the other 'February Pink'—both are earlier flowering than the type. Prunus *glandulosa sinensis* is a shrubby plant, always grown as a bush, and known as the Chinese Bush Cherry. It was very popular in Victorian and Edwardian times and is worth reviving because it is so easy to grow and gives a fine display in April. It gives a better performance if it is cut down hard every year, as soon as it has finished flowering. Prunus *padus* 'Watereri' is the Bird Cherry with a flower like a laurel, a spike sticking up from the branches as much as 8in long, with a delightful scent of almonds. The flowers of Prunus *sargentii* do not count as much as the leaves and the stem. The autumn colour is magnificent—bright orange red and the stem is shiny and attractive in its own right. Even so, the flowers are not to be despised—they are small, single pink and early. It is said to be the cherry most highly

H   121

favoured by the Japanese. In spite of its common name, The Spring Cherry—the most useful variety of Prunus *subhirtella* is the one that flowers in the autumn—Prunus *subhirtella autumnalis rosea*. Even this is an understatement because this tree will go on flowering throughout the winter, giving crop after crop of small, single pink flowers whenever the weather is kind. There is also an excellent weeping variety—Prunus *subhirtella pendula*—which is elegant and an excellent substitute for the weeping willow in a small garden.

Japanese Cherries: These trees are the Sato Zakura of Japan. They have all been raised in nurseries and private gardens and are of very mixed parentage. Most of them have double long-lasting flowers and a great many have an elegance of form and habit making them attractive in the winter.

Prunus 'Amanogawa' is the Lombardy Poplar Cherry. It grows as a narrow column producing, in the spring, large, fragrant semi-double pink flowers. The best known flowering cherry of all is Prunus 'Kanzan'. It is frequently planted as a street tree and some people object to its rather strong colour which is enhanced by bronze leaves. Even so, it is one of the most free flowering and decorative of all—provided you are not a purist and think the pink too harsh. The weeping cherry—Prunus 'Kiku-Shidare Zakura'—was known as 'Cheal's Weeping' for many years. It has a pendulous habit which is somewhat awkward to the point of being bizarre, yet beautiful because of it. The flowers are large, double and pink. Prunus 'Ukon' is a strange tree because it is the only yellow flowering cherry—and where the yellow colour came from nobody knows. It has the additional advantage of good autumn colour.

Peach: There is really only one flowering peach worth worrying about and that is Prunus *persica* 'Klara Mayer' (often spelt 'Clara Meyer'). The flowers are plentiful—neat little rosebuds of rich pink. It should be remembered that this is not a long lived tree and you will never see old and ancient specimens growing in gardens. But it is so good that, if it does begin to die back and die off, it is worth replacing with another.

Plum: Prunus *cerasifera* 'Pissardii', the dark leaved ornamental plum with small white flowers that are pink in bud, is one of the best known of all the ornamental flowering trees. It was discovered by a French gardener who was working for the Shah of Persia in 1880. The form called 'Nigra' has darker leaves and flowers that are rather more pink. Prunus 'Blireana' is a cross between this and one of the ornamental apricots. It, too, has purple leaves and double pink flowers which—to my mind—are among the most attractive of all the prunus family. It looks particularly well when planted with a tall growing forsythia, for it flowers at the same time, at the end of March and in early April.

Laurels: It seems a little odd to include laurels in a book which is concerned with ornamental plants, but Prunus *laurocerasus*, the Laurel, is seldom allowed to display its beauty, for it is almost always cut and clipped into the rigid shape of a hedge. There are two forms that are particularly good if they are allowed to grow as nature intended. Prunus *laurocerasus* 'Latifolia' has long dark green evergreen leaves and a very graceful habit of growth. If you wanted a really distinctive evergreen standard it is not much trouble to buy a young plant, cut it down to one stem, put a stick to it, and train it up, eventually to bush out at the top. A comparatively new form called Prunus *laurocerasus* 'Zebeliana' is low growing and wide spreading. The leaves are lighter in colour than those of Prunus *laurocerasus* 'Latifolia' and although they are evergreen they have the same shape as those of a willow. It is a good plant to grow under trees, and the narrow leaves make it valuable for flower arrangement. Prunus *lusitanicus* is the correct name of the Portugal Laurel which grows naturally into a rounded bush and makes an excellent specimen for a formal position. It will keep its neat habit without clipping.

The almonds, cherries, peaches and plums may all be grown as bush plants, half standards (on a 4–5ft stem) or full standards (6–7ft stem)— the exceptions are the Russian Almond (Prunus *tenella*) and the Chinese Bush Cherry (Prunus *glandulosa sinensis*) and—possibly—the Mount Fuji Cherry (Prunus *incisa*) which are all better grown as bush plants. Buy plants from a nursery or garden centre and set them at any time in open weather from October to March—but preferably in the autumn. The laurels are all grown and sold as bushes and are better plants in the early autumn or in the spring.

PURPLE

Some species and varieties of the following plants have purple flowers: Aster, Aubrieta, Buddleia, Crocus, Delphinium, Geranium, Hebe, Petunia, Phlox, Salvia, Syringa, Veronica.

PYRACANTHA—Firethorn

This evergreen shrub is often seen growing on walls, in spite of the fact that it makes a good bush on its own and—in some places where the soil suits it—a standard tree. It is an excellent evergreen and gives good winter colour in its berries. The flowers are white, rather like those of a May tree, and appear in May. Some varieties, like Pyracantha *atalantioides* (better known as Pyracantha 'Gibbsii') and Pyracantha 'Watereri' have copper-coloured young foliage—an added attraction. Both of these have orange-scarlet berries. Buy pot or container grown plants from a nursery or garden centre and set them at any time in open weather from October to April.

QUERCUS—The Oak

It seems unusual to include the Oak in a book which, nowadays, must of necessity be aimed at small gardens. But there are oaks and oaks. And one of the most useful small trees to be planted as a specimen, to provide shade and give colour in the autumn, is the Knaphill Scarlet Oak, Quercus *coccineus splendens*. It is true that it may take anything between five to ten years to become a significant specimen, but it will not grow out of hand very quickly. Its chief beauty is in its autumn colour—bright scarlet. What is more, the leaves hang on to the tree for a very long time giving a heart-warming display, particularly when winter is only just round the corner.

RANUNCULUS

The Ranunculus which are grown from bulbs are not the sort of plants that I would generally recommend, although they will go on flowering for several years, even when they are left in the ground. It is worth taking a chance on a mixed collection which should be planted in the autumn. But they fall down on the score of a continuous performance. The perennial varieties are far better because they are closely related to the buttercup—and you cannot have anything easier to grow than that. There are two varieties that are well worth planting, both with attractive common names. Ranunculus *aconitifolius fl. pl.* is called Fair Maids of France. It grows to about 18in, and flowers in May and June with neat little double white rosettes. It has been grown in this country since the days of the Tudors. Then there is Ranunculus *acris*, called Yellow Bachelor's Buttons, which is a little taller, at 2ft, flowering from June to August, often producing two crops, with small double yellow buttons. Buy plants from a nursery or garden centre and set them in the spring.

RED

Some species and varieties of the following plants have red flowers: Aster, Begonia, Camellia, Chaenomeles, Chrysanthemum, Crocosmia, Cytisus, Dianthus, Erica, Fuchsia, Geum, Gladiolus, Helianthemum, Lathyrus, Lilium, Lychnis, Malus, Paeonia, Papaver, Petunia, Phlox, Phygelius, Polyanthus, Ribes, Rose, Tropaeolum, Tulipa, Weigela.

RHEUM—Rhubarb

The ornamental varieties of the Rhubarb are very easy to grow and they are impressive plants. Rheum *palmatum atrosanguinea* has enormous leaves which are deeply cut and very attractive. It produces a red spike of flower which commands attention. Buy plants from a nursery or garden centre and set them in the autumn.

RHUS—Stagshorn Sumach

Rhus *typhina* grows anywhere—even in cities where the pollution is at its highest. It is one of the plants that became naturalised on bomb sites. It has big long leaves, a woolly stem, and it grows into an interesting shape, like a tree in an abstract painting, which makes it attractive even in the dead of winter. The leaves are like ferns and there is a variety called R. *t. laciniata* which has foliage that is more finely cut. Both of them make small trees or big bushes, up to 15ft in height, and they can be given the same treatment as the Tree of Heaven, Ailanthus *altissima*, by planting them in rich soil, keeping well fed, and cutting down every year to allow only two or three branches to develop. These then produce very long fronds of leaves which are tropical in their luxuriance. Buy plants from nursery or garden centre and set at any time in open weather from October to April.

RIBES—Flowering Currant

This is the well known spring flowering shrub with the unfortunate smell of cats. However, if it is admired at a distance, the smell can be ignored. There are two really good varieties—Ribes 'King Edward VII' is almost red and rather more compact in habit than the ordinary plant; Ribes 'Pulborough Scarlet', although not quite as bright in colour as the name suggests, has the added advantage of the flowers standing up better away from the stems. These are both very reliable shrubs of considerable beauty in the spring and the old flowering stems should be cut back as soon as the flowers are over. Buy plants from a nursery or garden centre and set them at any time in open weather from October to April.

ROBINIA—Common Acacia or The Black Locust

The ordinary varieties of this tree are far too large for the average garden and Robinia *pseudoacacia inermis*—the Mop-headed Acacia— has become too common as a street tree, giving its name to Acacia Avenue, to be desirable in the modern garden. But there is one which is the finest of all golden foliaged trees for the small garden. It is called Robinia *pseudoacacia* 'Frisia'. It does not grow too large but the chief advantage of it is that the foliage is bright gold and remains that colour throughout the summer. For it has to be realised that many golden foliaged plants soon become tarnished with age when the weather becomes hot and the dust begins to blow.

ROSA—Rose

It would be easy enough to say that all Roses qualify as good performance plants. This would not be strictly true because there are Roses for gardens, as there are horses for courses. Consequently, it is a little difficult to make specific recommendations as one Rose will grow well in one garden but not in another. Furthermore, there are some that grow in mine (like 'Spartan', a rich salmon-orange floribunda) which are now very difficult to obtain. Even so, there are a few which grow well almost anywhere—and some of them are as beautiful as they are easy-going.

The Species: There is a growing enthusiasm for the species roses, those that are natural plants, obtained from the wild. But there are not many of these that give the sort of show for the lack of care that is necessary to qualify them for this book. The following are the few that I can recommend.

Rosa *hugonis* grows to about 6ft and has arching sprays of neat foliage which are covered in yellow flowers in May. These are followed by small dark red hips—always provided there is not a May frost.

Rosa *moyesii* 'Geranium' has bright red flowers in June and July followed by dark red, pear-shaped hips in the autumn.

Rosa *rubrifolia* is worth growing simply for its coloured foliage. If the plant is in the sun it will be misty purple, if it is in the shade it will be grey-green, touched with mauve.

Hybrid Teas: Hybrid Tea roses are what most people understand by the name 'rose'. There are thousands still in cultivation, and all of them worth growing in some situation or other, for some purpose or other. The following is a list of well tried varieties, giving the reasons for their inclusion.

'Ena Harkness' is one of the finest of all red roses introduced at the end of World War II. It has a fault, it is true—that it is inclined to hang its head. But I have found, on a very light acid soil, that this does not apply. It is only when it is growing on ideal rose soil, and then puts on rather too much growth, that the trouble can be seen.

'Fragrant Cloud' is a rose of recent introduction with a fabulous scent as the name suggests. It is also a good bright red in the classic mould, able to win prizes at the shows of the Royal National Rose Society.

'Josephine Bruce'—another red rose which was raised and bred in Manchester. Consequently, it stands up well to a wet summer.

'Peace' (see page 88). This is *the* rose. It is so strong growing that nothing can destroy it. But because it is so vigorous, it needs only light pruning if it is to produce its yellow flowers, lightly shaded with pink at their best. It will grow anywhere, easily, for anyone.

'Peer Gynt'. A comparatively new rose which might almost be described as a 'Shrub Rose'. It is a vigorous plant which throws strong branches that hold bunches of flowers in yellow touched with pink at the edges.

'Perfecta'. One of the best of all bicolors. It has shades of pink and silver and yellow.

'Piccadilly'. Another bicolor, a mixture of bright vermilion red and yellow with a deep yellow reverse. It is very free flowering and strong in growth.

'Pink Favourite' is one of the best of all pink hybrid teas. It is a strong growing bush that will grow as high as 6 or 8ft if it is only pruned lightly. Unfortunately, like all pink roses, it has little or no scent.

'Rose Gaujard'. In spite of the fact that it was raised in the South of France, 'Rose Gaujard' stands up to our normal wet English summers very well indeed. It is a delightful mixture of silver and rich pink— silver on the outside of the petals and pink on the inside.

'Sterling Silver'. The search for a blue rose still goes on. But, so far, it has not been found. On the way, several good varieties have been introduced which are in shades of mauve and lilac. This is one of the blue near-misses—and very attractive too.

'Super Star'. Next to 'Peace', this rose is one of the outstanding introductions of recent years. It has brilliant vermilion flowers but, what is even more important, it will grow almost anywhere—I have had it growing in the shade of an elm tree (before the Dutch elm disease began to kill them) and it was even able to compete with the roots of that voracious feeder.

'Virgo'. The best white hybrid tea that is grown today—although there is still room for the very old 'Frau Karl Drushki' which might be better classified as a shrub rose because it can be left to grow on its own.

The Floribunda Roses: These are the rose bushes that produce heads of flowers, in trusses. Mostly they are semi-double and they are vigorous plants that are better for not being pruned too hard.

'Allgold'. An excellent rose, for it has the great virtue of being impervious to disease. It is a good yellow and free flowering while the foliage is bright and shiny and a vigorous shade of green.

'Anne Cocker'. A new floribunda rose in deep red on good foliage which is almost purple. It has the considerable advantage of lasting a long time when cut.

'Dearest'. A delightful shade of soft salmon pink with strong growth and foliage. It goes on flowering for a long time and has a good scent.

'Iceberg'. Perhaps the finest of all the floribundas for performance. This is a white rose with, sometimes, just the faintest tinge of pink in the bud. It is fragrant, free flowering and grows well.

'Masquerade'. One of the sensational roses. When this rose first appeared with its red and yellow flowers and red flowers and yellow flowers all on the same bush, the experts prophesied that it would only be an oddity. But it has proved to be so good for general garden use that it is now deservedly one of the most popular of all.

'Queen Elizabeth'. A strong growing floribunda rose reaching as high as 8ft, if it is left to grow, and it still flowers then without any attention. A good pink and a large flower.

'Orange Sensation'. This rose appears to be more orange because of the touch of vermilion in its colour. It has a scent, it grows well and the foliage is dark green.

Climbers: Climbing roses have been developed as much as any of the others in the last twenty years. There are several good perpetual flowering varieties—yet some of the old stagers are still worth growing.

'Albertine'. This is an old rambler rose, a one-shot plant, but of such a delightful shade of light coppery pink that it is well qualified to be listed. Seen at its best climbing through an old apple tree, or something similar.

'Danse de Feu'. This is one of the new perpetual flowering climbers, a brilliant red which goes on throughout the summer.

'Pink Perpetué'. A good pink perpetual flowerer.

'Ritter von Barmstede'. A double pink, and continuous flowering.

'Zephyrine Drouhin'. The thornless rose, salmon pink flowers—may also be grown as a shrub, or bush rose.

Shrub Roses: The shrub roses have been defined as the floribundas that you don't prune—or they could equally well be some of the modern climbers which you do prune. The result is a big flowering shrub which goes on giving colour throughout the summer.

'Ballerina'. A dainty rose with small pink flowers and plenty of them.

'Fred Loads'. Bright orange scarlet, single flowers, glowing with colour.

'Schoolgirl'. Enormous single flowers in a charming shade of pink touched with yellow.

There are many old-fashioned shrub roses which have considerable charm. But they have the disadvantage of only giving one show of flowers and they need a lot of space to do that. Consequently, I do not list them here as I do not think their performance justifies the room they need.

All roses may be bought from nurseries or garden centres, either open ground or container grown, or even from supermarkets and other stores in polythene packs. They may be planted at any time in open weather from November to March.

ROSEMARINUS *officinalis*—Rosemary

This delightful shrub, which is as valuable in the garden for its scented grey-green foliage and blue flowers in April and May as it is in the kitchen for flavouring, grows to between 6 and 8ft—and it has been cultivated in this country for more than 400 years. It flowers in May and can be planted almost anywhere, in a shrub border, mixed border, the herb garden or as a specimen on its own. There is a curious super-stition about Rosemary which I have found to be more or less true. It is said that you should never buy it—but that it should be given to you. I bought two on one occasion, gave one to my next door neighbour which thrived—and planted one myself, which died. But if you cannot

Rudbeckia Laciniata

persuade some kind friend or relation to give you one, then buy a pot or container grown plant from a nursery or garden centre and set it in the spring.

RUBUS—Bramble

It seems unlikely to plant a Bramble in the garden and you would not saddle yourself with the common wild variety on purpose. But there is one which is singularly beautiful in winter in having fine purple stems covered with a whiter than white bloom. This makes it distinctive enough to make friends start up and say—'What's that?' The name of this plant with the beautiful stems is Rubus *cockburnianus*, although it is probably still better known by its older name of *giraldianus*. Buy plants from a nursery or garden centre, set them at any time in open weather from October to April—and cut the stems down hard every year as soon as they have finished flowering.

RUDBECKIA—Cone Flower

Another very strong perennial which grows anywhere and it is very hard to kill. It has big yellow daisylike flowers surrounding a tall black cone in the centre, which gives the flower its name. It is a useful plant for giving a bit of height to a border in August and September. It needs no staking and is excellent for cutting. Even when the flowers are over, the black cone remains looking rather like a miniature bullrush, and it can still be used effectively in the flower vases. The toughest of them all is Rudbeckia *laciniata*, growing to between 5 and 8ft, 'Autumn Sun' is similar, but deeper in colour, and R. *nitida* 'Herbstsonne' has petals that hang down and show off the cone to advantage. 'Goldsturm' or 'Sullivant's Variety' is a much shorter plant, reaching only 3ft and, 'Goldquelle' is a deep yellow, semi-double at the same height. Buy plants from a nursery or garden centre and set them at any time in open weather between November and March.

RUTA—Rue

Shakespeare's 'Sour Herb of Grace'. There is little use for this herb in cooking although, I am told, it makes a very good rinse after washing the hair—but it is invaluable in the garden for ground cover. There is only one variety worth bothering about—Ruta *graveolens* 'Jackman's

Blue', found by Mr Rowland Jackman in a cottage garden in Addle-
stone in Surrey. It has neat grey-green leaves which are covered with
a glaucous sheen. It makes excellent ground cover, up to about 15in,
and will grow almost anywhere. Buy pot or container grown plants
from a nursery or garden centre and set them in the spring.

SAGE—see Salvia

SALVIA
The best of all the Salvias is the Common Sage, Salvia *officinalis*. It is a
shrub that is used mostly for cooking but it is very beautiful when it is
in full flower at the end of June, growing to about 2½ft. Unfortunately,
it is seldom seen at its best because if it is allowed to flower the foliage
deteriorates and is not so good for flavouring stuffings and stews.
Consequently, it is wise to have two plants—one for show and one for
the pot which should never be allowed to flower.

There are also several very good perennial forms of the Salvia.
Salvia *superba* grows to about 2ft with reddish-purple flowers made up
of a red calyx and violet-coloured petals. It dies very gracefully
because the red calyces remain behind to give colour after the petals
have dropped. There is a more dwarf form called 'Lubeca' growing to
2ft with similar coloured flowers. These have nothing to do with those
nasty red half-hardy Salvias, which stretch in endless lines across the
country throughout the summer. Buy the shrubby form, Salvia
officinalis, from a garden centre where you will usually find it in the
herb section and it must be pot or container grown. Buy the herbaceous
varieties—*superba* and 'Lubeca'—also from garden centres or nurseries
and set them at any time in open weather from the end of January to
early April.

SAMBUCUS—Elder
Like the Bramble, it would seem to be unlikely to plant this common
shrub in a garden. But the golden form of the Common Elder (Sambucus *nigra foliis aurea*) is one of the best golden foliaged shrubs that can
be grown. The reason for this is that it continues to make young
growth throughout the summer and always looks fresh, rather like
Robinia 'Frisia'. It is an inexpensive plant to buy and very easy to grow.

Buy plants from a nursery or garden centre and set them at any time in open weather from November to March.

SANTOLINA *chamaecyparissus*—French Lavender or Cotton Lavender
This is a good ground cover plant with grey foliage, which is its chief asset. The flowers are yellow bobbles and not very attractive. It should be clipped down hard in the spring every year—and I would clip off the flowers, too, as soon as they begin to show. Buy plants from a nursery or garden centre, open ground or container grown, and set them in the spring—March or April.

SARCOCOCCA *hookeriana*—Digyna
This seems an outlandish name to be included in a book which is only concerned with plants that give a good performance and grow any-where—but this winter flowering shrub will do just that. It grows to about 3ft with long slender branches carrying evergreen leaves, rather like those of a willow. About the middle of January it begins to open its flowers which have a most delicious scent—provided they are sniffed at a distance outside. If they are brought into the house, they are over-powering and can, on occasions, resemble the smell of stables. I have been told that it grows particularly well in the middle of a group of Montbretia. I tried this, once but—I fear-—without success, which may have been more my fault than the plant's. Buy plants from a nursery or garden centre and set them at any time in open weather from November to April.

SAXIFRAGA—Saxifrage
These are the well known rock plants, but the old London Pride or St Patrick's Cabbage (Saxifraga *umbrosa*) is still an excellent edging for a border. Not only are the dainty pink flowers, up to about 9 or 12in, very attractive, but the foliage is also neat and tidy after they are over. There are an infinite number of saxifrages, it is the largest section in the Royal Horticultural Society's *Dictionary of Gardening*, but the mossy types are the best for general use—on the rock garden, in sink gardens, in the interstices of crazy paving and in almost any odd spot. 'Pixie' is pink, 'Carnival' is deeper and, somewhat obviously, 'White Pixie' is

white. They flower in April and May. Buy plants, which must be pot grown, from a nursery or garden centre and set them in the spring.

SCILLA—Squill

These are miniature bulbs which produce small blue flowers with an intensity of colouring that is almost staggering. They can be grown near trees and in grass—two characteristics that make them useful indeed. They flower at the same time as the Snowdrops, and the two look very well together. There are several different kinds—S. *bifolia* is the cheapest, with good blue flowers, S. *siberica* 'Spring Beauty' is larger but more expensive, and the best but most expensive is S. 'Tubergeniana' which throws three or four spikes to a bulb, with china blue flowers that have a turquoise stripe on the back of the petal.

SCREENING

Some of the species and varieties of the following plants are suitable for screening eyesores, of one sort or another, in one way or another: Actinidia, Chamaecyparis, Corylus, Cotoneaster, Cupressocyparis, Elaeagnus, Helianthus, Ilex, Juniperus, Ligustrum, Picea, Prunus (Laurel), Pyracantha, Tropaeolum.

SEDUM—Stonecrop

The chief attraction of the Stonecrop is its foliage. It is rather like a form of land seaweed with little bubbly leaves. There are three different colours available—S. 'Coral Carpet' is pink, S. 'Cautocolum' has silver leaves and pink flowers from September to October, and S. *spathuli-folium purpureum* is attractive with purple leaves covered in a grey bloom. All these are the well known small creeping plants. Then there is the Ice Plant which is rather taller—Sedum *spectabile*. The best variety to grow is Sedum *spectabile* 'Autumn Joy' because this has dark red flowers which last right through the late summer and early autumn, fading into attractive seed heads. Buy plants from a nursery or garden centre and set them in the spring. The smaller leaved varieties should be pot grown.

SENECIO—Groundsel

The common name of one of our less popular weeds is no indication of the beauty of two of the most attractive Groundsels for the garden. Senecio *greyii* is one of our best grey-foliaged shrubs. The flowers are not particularly attractive, because they do resemble those of the common Groundsel and it is better to keep them clipped off. Incidentally, the more you cut this plant back the better it likes it. It grows into a much more bushy specimen and is hardier. Buy this from a nursery or garden centre, it must be pot or container grown, and plant it in the spring. Senecio *cineraria*, as it is now called, is, strictly speaking, a bedding plant grown entirely for its bright silver foliage. It looks as if it might be an exciting fern from outer space, but it is rather more homely than that—for it has become naturalised in many parts of the British Isles. Consequently buy and plant out Cineraria *maritima* (the name by which it is still much better known) in accordance with the time/place scale given on page 16 and plant with discretion. You may well find that some of the plants will survive the winter in your garden and become permanently established as semi-shrubs about 2½ft high and 3ft across. They may succumb in a really hard winter but they stand a good chance of living for three or four years. When this happens, Cineraria *maritima* becomes one of the best of all performance plants, from both points of view. You can then plan your planting around these silver beauties, and save money by not having to obtain fresh plants every spring. Buy bedding plants, preferably pot grown, in the first instance—plant them at the right time for the right place—and see what happens after that.

SEPTEMBER

Some species and varieties of the following plants flower in September: Anemone, Aster, Begonia, Calendula, Ceratostigma, Chrysanthemum, Colchicum, Cortaderia, Crocosmia, Crocus, Elaeagnus, Fatsia, Fuchsia, Geranium, Hebe, Hibiscus, Hydrangea, Hypericum, Lavatera, Leycesteria, Lobularia, Petunia, Phygelius, Physalis, Polygonum, Potentilla, Rose, Rudbeckia, Sedum, Solidago, Spartium, Spiraea, Tamarix, Topaeolum.

SHORT

Some of the species and varieties of the following plants are short growing, reaching no more than 1ft or 15in at the most:

Annuals: Echium, Lobularia, Myosotis, Petunia, Tropaeolum.

Bulbs: Begonia, Crocosmia, Crocus, Galanthus, Muscari, Narcissus, Scilla.

Perennials: Alchemilla, Alyssum, Aubrieta, Bergenia, Centaurea, Dianthus, Iris, Lamium, Lychnis, Mentha, Nepeta, Oenothera, Origanum, Phlox, Primula, Saxifraga, Stachys.

Shrubs: Contoneaster, Erica, Genista, Hebe, Heliantheum, Hypericum, Juniper, Potentilla, Ruta, Santolina, Vinca.

SKIMMIA

The Skimmia is an evergreen berry-bearing shrub but it does have a rather complicated sex life. The well known Skimmia *japonica* and a similar plant called Skimmia *reevesiana* need to have both male and female plants if the females are to set berries. However, there is now a variety of Skimmia *japonica* called 'Redruth' which has male and female flowers all on the same bush. At the present time, this is only obtainable from Southdown Nurseries, Redruth, Cornwall. Another attractive skimmia is a dwarf form called Skimmia *japonica* 'Rubella'. This does not bear berries very freely but it has the considerable charm of holding its buds throughout the winter which look as if they are just about to burst open. It only grows to about 2ft high and is useful for winter decoration. This can be obtained from most nurseries or garden centres and may be bought either as a container shrub or from the open ground, to be planted in the spring.

SNOWDROP—see Galanthus

SOLIDAGO—Golden Rod—or Aaron's Rod

This is a rough and tough plant which has become naturalised in many places and is one of those perennials that survives years of neglect. The old-fashioned sorts are not particularly beautiful, in fact they might almost be described as ugly. But there are now many good varieties. My own favourite is 'Goldenmosa' which grows to about $2\frac{1}{2}$-3ft and flowers in late August with small blossoms which are similar to those of the 'Mimosa' (Acacia) which are always on sale early in the year in florists' shops. Another good sort is 'Loddon' which grows taller, at about 3½ft, and has bright-yellow flowers in July. 'Wendy' is dwarf and compact, flowering later in August and September. All of them are excellent on their own but they also make a good foil to the Michaelmas Daisies. Buy plants from a nursery or garden centre and set them in the spring.

SORBUS—Mountain Ash and Service Tree

Sorbus *aucuparia* is the common Mountain Ash. It has the advantage of giving early colour from its berries in August. The only trouble is that, although these are decorative, they are depressing because they are an early reminder of autumn—and winter not far behind. There are several others that are good for smaller gardens because they do not grow as strongly as the native plant. Sorbus *cashmiriana*, from Kashmir, has white berries which stay long on the trees because birds do not touch white berries unless they are very hard pressed. Sorbus *vilmorinii* has fernlike leaves which turn red and purple in the autumn, and pink berries later becoming white. Sorbus *aria* is the Service Tree with white young leaves, but the best form is Sorbus *aria lutescens* which expands its buds in brightest silver and the effect in early May is as good as many flowers. All the sorbus are best grown as half standards or standard trees and may be bought from nurseries and garden centres, either as open ground plants or in containers, and set at any time in open weather from the end of October to the end of March.

SPARTIUM *junceum*—Spanish Broom

The Spanish Broom (see page 69) grows to a height of about 6 or 8ft. It needs to be pruned hard in the spring. You can even time its flowering by pruning. If it is cut back early, then it will start to flower in June or July and go on until August or September—or you can delay it a little, when it will continue flowering until the frosts. Buy plants, which must be pot or container grown, from a nursery or garden centre and set them at any time in open weather from October to April.

SPECIMEN PLANTS

Some species and varieties of the following flowering trees and shrubs make good specimen plants—some as bushes, some as standards or half standards—to be planted on their own in a prominent position: Ailanthus, Amelanchier, Aucuba, Betula, Camellia, Chamaecyparis, Cistus, Cornus, Cortaderia, Corylus, Cotoneaster, Cupressocyparis, Eleagnus, Erica, Fatsia, Forsythia, Hamamelis, Hibiscus, Ilex, Juniperus, Laburnum, Ligustrum, Liquidamber, Magnolia, Malus, Olearia, Osmanthus, Phyllyrea, Prunus, Quercus, Rhus, Robinia, Rosemary, Sorbus, Syringa, Tamarix, Viburnum, Yucca.

Among the perennials, both Macleaya and Rheum make handsome clumps in isolation.

SPIRAEA

There are many different forms of Spiraea with different common names. One of the most attractive of all is called both 'Bridal Wreath' and 'Foam of May'—its correct Latin name is Spiraea *arguta*. It has small, light-green leaves, which are useful for decoration even when the flowers are over, and a mass of tiny white flowers in April. Spiraea *thunbergii* is very similar but rather smaller, both in its growth—up to about 3 or 4ft against Spiraea *arguta*'s 5–8ft—and with smaller leaves and smaller flowers. Spiraea *japonica* 'Anthony Waterer' is a different plant altogether. It grows to about 2 or 3ft and should be cut down every year in the spring. It then produces whorls of red flowers in July and August. If these, too, are cut off as soon as they are over, the late flush of young growth is attractively variegated in silver and pink. One of the tallest of Spiraeas that may be a little difficult to find, but is well worth growing, is Spiraea *prunifolia* which not only carries double white flowers in the spring, but has very good coloured foliage in the autumn. It grows to about 8ft. All of these shrubs should be bought from a nursery or garden centre, either open ground or container grown, and set at any time in open weather from the end of October to the end of March.

STACHYS *lanatum*—Lamb's Ears

This dwarf growing plant, only reaching 1ft in height at most, has woolly grey leaves which make it singularly attractive for ground cover and for use in the flower vase. The red flowers appear in July, but as they are largely covered by the leaves they are comparatively insignificant. Buy plants from a nursery or garden centre, preferably pot or container grown and set them in the spring.

STONECROP—see Sedum

SWEET PEA—see Lathyrus *odoratum*

SWEET WILLIAM—see Dianthus

SYRINGA—Lilac

There is always some confusion between the Lilac and the Mock Orange, to use the common names, or between the *Syringa* and the *Philadelphus*, to use the Latin names. The reason is that when both first came to this country they were called the Persian Pipestem Tree because the wood of both was hollowed out and used for that purpose. The correct name of the *Lilac* is the *Syringa* and it is a shrub which has been grown here for so long as almost to appear to be a native plant—it is certainly naturalised in some places. Even the old common Syringa *vulgaris*, the small flowered species in pale lilac mauve is decorative when it is in flower. There are many excellent varieties, some of the new sorts are quite startling—there is even a yellow—but the old tried and trusted sorts are still the best for general performance. Among the singles are 'Congo', a dark purple and one that still stands out in a collection of lilacs; 'Souvenir de Louis Spath' is a single near-red. Probably the finest of all the doubles is 'Madame Lemoine', a white, which has a beautiful scent and is still used for forcing cut flowers. It behaves extremely well in the garden. There is also 'Charles Joly', a good double red. These are all best grown as bushes, reaching about 8 or 10ft when they are mature. There is one important point about buying plants—they should be on their own roots. Quite often, Lilacs are grafted on privet and they are unsatisfactory—more so if they are grafted on to the common type, Syringa *vulgaris*, because then the suckers cannot be distinguished from the true plant. Buy plants from a nursery or garden centre, which may either be open ground or container grown, but if you can, check that they do not have any union showing that will indicate they have been grafted or budded in the same way as a rose bush. Set them at any time in open weather from the end of October to the end of March.

TAGETES

African marigolds and French marigolds are both forms of tagetes, which is a Mexican plant, well known to the Aztecs, but neither of them has anything to do with Africa or France. Today there are many different forms which are best bought as bedding out plants, although some of the best, the 'Climax' strain of African marigolds, can be treated as hardy annuals in the milder parts of the country. Buy plants, which should be set out in accordance with the table on page 16, or buy a packet of seeds and take a chance on sowing in the open—but not before the middle of May.

TALL

Species and varieties of the following plants are tall growing—from 4ft upwards.

Annuals: Helianthus.

Bulbs: Lilium.

Perennials: Anchusa, Aster, Delphinium, Digitalis, Echinops, Filipendula, Galega, Helianthus, Inula, Iris, Lathyrus, Macleaya, Rheum, Rudbeckia, Solidago, Verbascum.

Trees and Shrubs: Ailanthus, Amelanchier, Aucuba, Berberis, Betula, Buddleia, Camellia, Chamaecyparis, Cortaderia, Corylus, Cotoneaster, Cupressocyparis, Cytisus, Eleagnus, Escallonia, Euonymus, Fatsia, Filipendula, Forsythia, Garrya, Hamamelis, Ilex, Juniperus, Kerria, Laburnum, Leycesteria, Ligustrum, Liquidamber, Osmanthus, Philadelphus, Phillyrea, Prunus, Quercus, Rhus, Robinia, Rose, Sorbus, Spartium, Spiraea, Syringa, Viburnum, Weigela.

TAMARIX—Tamarisk

One species of this shrub is native to the British Isles and it grows wild in seaside places where it acts as an excellent windbreak. But for garden purposes two alone are necessary—Tamarix *pentandra* and Tamarix *tetrandra*. Tamarix *tetrandra*, the last in the alphabet, is the first to flower. It blooms in May with long plumes of rich pink flowers which are produced on the old wood. Consequently, it should be cut back as soon as it has finished flowering. Tamarix *pentandra*, the first in the alphabet, is the last to flower. It blooms in August with, if anything, rather longer sprays than Tamarix *tetrandra* from the wood made in that season. Therefore, this species should be cut back every year early in the spring. There is a good new variety called 'Pink Cascade' which has still longer sprays of flowers. Buy plants, either open ground or container grown, from a nursery or garden centre, and set them at any time in open weather from the end of October to the end of March.

THYMUS—Thyme

Another herb that is as decorative as it is tasty. But apart from its use in the kitchen, it is useful to plant on rock gardens, at the edges of borders and particularly in the interstices of crazy paving or any paving. When it is walked upon and crushed in hot weather, the scent is delightful. There are many varieties, some with different scents but the straight Thyme is probably the best—colours can be varied in the flowers that come out in June and July. Thymus *serpyllum coccineum* is red, 'Pink Chintz' is pink—and there are several more, white and in the varying shades of mauve of the natural plant. Buy plants from a nursery or garden centre which must be pot or container grown and set them in the spring.

TROPAEOLUM—Nasturtium—Indian Cress—*The* Plant of the book

The Nasturtium is so easy to cultivate that it is often the first flower grown by children, just as radishes are their first vegetable. It is so easy it might almost stand a chance of being left out because it really does prefer the very poorest soil. Consequently, it is excellent for growing on the roots of trees, or up into a privet hedge, or right against early flowering shrubs, like forsythia, to give them colour during the summer. It can also be used trained over a wire fence to give cover and flower during the first season in a new garden. The best known nasturtiums are the Golden Gleam hybrids which were first introduced into this country in 1931, when they were the sensation of the Chelsea Flower Show. They were found in California, growing in the garden of a small house, by the well known American seedsman, Mr J. C. Bodger. He was never able to discover the true origin, although the owner of the garden said they had come from Mexico. There are several different forms of this particular strain—Golden Gleam,

Tropaeolum

Scarlet Gleam, Gleam Hybrids, which are mixed in colour, and other different strains vary in their ability to climb and this should be checked on the seed packet. There is also another form called Mixed Tall Single which is a very strong climber but not quite as showy. Dwarf Nasturtiums are now being raised so that the flowers are held above the leaves. 'Cherry Rose' is a semi-double, 'Talisman' is new, in the same form but a much darker colour, while 'Salmon Baby' is the colour of its name. These grow to about 1ft high by about 1ft across. Leaves of the Nasturtium can be used in salads—some people even make sandwiches of them alone—they have a strong mustard taste. I have been told that the seeds can be used as a substitute for capers, but I have never tried this myself and would therefore not like to recommend it. Buy a packet of seeds and put them in with your finger, about ½in deep, at any time from the middle of March to the middle of May.

VERBASCUM—Mullein
This wild plant of the British Isles is one of the most adaptable in the book. It will grow and seed itself in almost any soil. Strictly speaking, it is a biennial—which means, as explained in the beginning of the book, that you sow the seeds one year to flower the next. However, the seeds will sow themselves and grow into good plants which may be transplanted as required. Incidentally, it is so tough that it is, in my experience, the only plant that is completely impervious to the effects of paraquat weedkillers (eg Weedol). The two native varieties are Verbascum blattaria, the Moth Mullein, and Verbascum nigrum, the Dark Mullein. There is not much difference between the two—they grow to anything up to 7 or 8ft giving tall spikes of yellow flowers which go on and on throughout the summer. As this is a very common plant, it might be difficult to find seed. The only thing to do is to find a friend who has some and ask him to give it to you, or perhaps find a wild stand (these occur more often on chalk than on other soils) and collect seed and sow it in your garden. The species Vervascum vernale in some catalogues is, in fact, Verbascum nigrum, so if all else fails—buy plants of this from a nursery or garden centre and set them in the spring. There are also a number of cultivated perennial varieties which are not as tall as the wild forms. 'Gainsborough' is a yellow, 'Rose Bouquet' is pink and 'Bridal Bouquet' is white. All these grow to

about 4ft. Buy plants from a nursery or garden centre and set them in the spring.

VERONICA—Speedwell

These are excellent perennials for the late summer in varying shades of blue and purple—a time when this colour is not over plentiful. But do not be misled by some that are described as 'pink' or 'red purple'. These are travesties of the original and it is better to keep to the true blue colour and take the best that the Speedwells can give. All the varieties grow to between 1 and 2ft high and are excellent for the front of the border, where they look particularly well against gaillardias, both in the contrast of colour and the different shapes of the flowers. Three of the best varieties are 'Wendy', 'True Blue' and 'Blue Peter'. Buy plants from a nursery or garden centre and set them in the spring.

VIBURNUM

There is no common name which covers the whole of the viburnums, which is not surprising seeing that they are so varied and so beautiful. They provide a range of deciduous and evergreen flowering shrubs which give flower and scent throughout the year. The most popular of all, at one time, was Viburnum *carlesii*—and I only mention it because it is so well known. In my experience, it does not qualify for this book because in recent years it has suffered from a curious ailment which has caused the buds to dry up and fall off before the flowers open. Furthermore, it is very prone to attacks of black fly. The following is a list of the best, and they are all good performance plants:

Viburnum 'Burkwoodii': An evergreen flowering shrub which will grow as high as 10ft or it may be trained up a wall. The leaves are glossy green, it flowers in May, opening as pink buds developing to white rosettes which are deliciously scented.

Viburnum *farrerii*: This shrub is still far better known as Viburnum *fragrans*—the name under which it was grown from its introduction at the end of the last century until quite recently. It is the best of all the winter flowering shrubs. It starts to open its pink buds in November.

They develop to pale pink flowers, eventually turning white. These go on until February or even March. The earlier name—*fragrans*—is the most descriptive because this shrub has one of the strongest scents in the garden. It is also handsome when flowering is over, for the leaves are bronzy green and add distinction to any mixed border.

Viburnum *opulus*—Guelder Rose: A native plant which is very strong growing and will even make a small tree 10 or 12ft high. Although it is seen in many a hedgerow, it is very decorative in its flat open flowers in May which are followed by bunches of glistening red fruits and bright autumn colour in the leaves. Fortunately, there is now a more dwarf variety, suitable for smaller gardens. This is called Viburnum *opulus compactum* and it has all the same characteristics as its big brother. A word of warning—have nothing to do with Viburnum *opulus nanum*, which is a different plant, ugly, a malformed dwarf which does not flower.

Viburnum *opulus sterile*—Snowball Tree: This is a variation of the common plant which does not berry but, as compensation, it carries big white balls of flower that give it the common name of Snowball Tree. It does have the advantage of giving good autumn colour and it is not quite so strong growing as Viburnum *opulus*. Gertrude Jekyll liked to grow this shrub with a plant of Clematis *montana rubens* climbing through its branches.

Viburnum *plicatum*—Japanese Snowball Tree: This species has rather more grace and charm than our own snowball tree, particularly in the formation of its flowers. It is also more compact in habit and more suited to smaller gardens. Unfortunately, it has no scent but the flowers in late May or early June are very decorative, like miniature hydrangeas.

Viburnum *plicatum* 'Mariesii': The habit of this plant is one of its chief attractions—it grows as a rounded shrub in layers, spreading outwards and upwards. It is very free flowering and when it is in full flower in May and June, it looks as if it were covered in snow. Like some of the other deciduous varieties of the viburnum, it also has good autumn colour and, in a hot summer, red berries which eventually turn black.

Viburnum *rhytidophyllum*: The most handsome of all the evergreen viburnums—for its leaves. It grows to a big bush, 10 or 12ft high, and the long leathery deeply-veined leaves hang down in dark green with the underside covered in a brown bloom. The flowers develop in the autumn as buds which last through the winter, giving a promise of the beauty to come, and they open as creamy white circles in May. The fruits are particularly attractive and are more freely borne than in some of the other species. Like those of Viburnum *plicatum* 'Mariesii', they start red and turn black. Altogether a very impressive plant.

Viburnum *tinus*—Laurestinus: One of our oldest evergreens which suffers from having been included in that rather murky form of planting—the Victorian shrubbery. Even so, it is a good evergreen and a good winter flowering plant. The leaves are small, glossy green, and the flowers open as pink buds turning to white—they will often start, like Viburnum *farrerii*, in November and go on until the spring. There is one particularly good variety called V. *t.* 'Eve Price' which is smaller in growth—reaching about 6 or 8ft against the laurestinus' eventual 10 by 15ft, or even more.

Buy plants from a nursery or garden centre (V. *tinus* is better if it is container grown) and set them at any time in open weather from October to March.

VINCA—Periwinkle

The Periwinkle has been grown here for so long that nobody is quite sure whether it is native or not. There are two forms—V. *major* and V. *minor*. V. *major* is a good plant for ground cover. It grows strongly with long tendrils and big leaves that will quickly cover a bank. It has large, rather pale, blue flowers which appear spasmodically throughout the summer. The best of all for flower is Vinca *minor* 'Bowles Variety'. This is a charming small plant which really does go on flowering all the time, producing crop after crop of bright blue flowers. The leaves are small, consequently it is not quite as good for ground cover as its larger counterpart, but the colour is a very delicate shade of blue. The plants should be cut back in the early spring to encourage them to grow and flower. Buy plants from a nursery or garden centre, which may either be open ground or pot grown, and set them at any time from the end of October to the end of March.

VITIS—Vine

There are many ornamental vines and some are more easy to grow than others. I feel that only one really comes up to the standard of this book—Vitis *coignetiae*. This is a strong growing plant which produces enormous leaves that are heart shaped at the base. These turn a brilliant colour in the autumn—orange and scarlet. It is a plant that can be left to ramble over an old tree or an old building—and it can even be used as ground cover to grow over the parts where spring bulbs have died down after flowering. Buy plants from a nursery or garden centre, they must be pot or container grown, and set them in the autumn or in the spring.

WEIGELA

This good flowering shrub has suffered at the hands of the botanists more than most. First it was Weigela, then it was Diervilla (and may still be found under this name) and now, once again, it is Weigela. It is a very easy shrub to grow and the original plant, Weigela *florida*, was found by Robert Fortune in a mandarin's garden in Canton in 1845. There are now many excellent hybrids and the best are Weigela *florida variegata*, a silver variegated form which is singularly decorative throughout the summer, carrying pale pink flowers in May and June backed by silver variegated leaves. Weigela 'Abel Carriere', is a shrub that may be a little difficult to obtain but it does have very attractive salmon-pink flowers. There are two good red varieties— Weigelas 'Eve Rathke' and 'Bristol Ruby' and there is not much to choose between the two. With the exception of Weigela *florida variegata*, they should all be pruned back hard as soon as they have finished flowering. Weigela *florida variegata* is not so strong growing and only needs dead wood cutting out, leaving the stronger shoots. Buy plants from a nursery or garden centre which may either be open ground or container grown and set them at any time from the end of October to the end of March.

WHITE

Some species and varieties of the following plants have white flowers: Achillea, Amelanchier, Anemone, Aster, Buddleia, Camellia, Campanula, Centaurea, Chrysanthemum, Cistus, Crocus, Cytisus, Delphinium, Deutzia, Dianthus, Erica, Fatsia, Filipendula, Galanthus, Gypsophila, Hibiscus, Hydrangea, Iris, Jasmine, Lathyrus, Lilium, Lobularia, Lunaria, Lupinus, Magnolia, Narcissus, Olearia, Osmanthus, Paeonia, Papaver, Petunia, Philadelphus, Phlox, Polygonatum, Polygonum, Potentilla, Prunus, Pyracantha, Ranunculus, Rose, Sarcococca, Spiraea, Syringa, Verbascum, Viburnum, Yucca.

YELLOW

Some species and varieties of the following plants have yellow flowers: Achillea, Alchemilla, Alyssum, Begonia, Berberis, Calendula, Coreopsis, Crocus, Cytisus, Doronicum, Euphorbia, Forsythia, Gaillardia, Garrya, Genista, Gladiolus, Hamamelis, Helianthemum, Helianthus, Hemerocallis, Hypericum, Inula, Jasminum, Kerria, Laburnum, Ligularia, Lonicera, Lupinus, Mahonia, Narcissus, Oenothera, Potentilla, Primula, Prunus (Cerasus 'Ukon' only), Ranunculus, Rose, Santolina, Senecio, Solidago, Spartium, Tagetes, Ulex, Verbascum.

YUCCA—Adam's Needle

The Yucca suffers from a bad reputation—that it only flowers once every seven years. However, this is an old wives'—or rather—old gardeners' tale because many plants have been known to flower every year. The foliage consists of a spray of handsome swordlike leaves and from the centre of this, in July and August, there appears a tall spike of white flowers which are somewhat similar to those of the lily—to which the plant is related. There are two main species—Yucca *filamentosa* and Yucca *gloriosa*. Yucca *filamentosa* has small 'filaments' growing from the sides of the leaves, and there is a variegated form. Yucca *gloriosa* is rather stronger growing and the flowers are very similar, reaching as high as 6ft. Again—there is a variegated form which is perhaps rather more attractive than that of Yucca *filamentosa*. Both these are good flowering plants but it should be remembered that one of their chief advantages is in their form and foliage, both of which have a subtropical effect. Incidentally, there is a singularly good flowering variety called Yucca *flaccida* 'Ivory', which has recently been selected. It has big flowers of creamy white, slightly touched with green. Buy plants from a nursery or garden centre and set them at any time from October to March.